# STORY-WORSHIP PROGRAMS
## FOR THE CHURCH SCHOOL YEAR

### REV. JAY S. STOWELL, M.A.

# STORY-WORSHIP PROGRAMS
## FOR THE
# CHURCH SCHOOL YEAR

BY

## REV. JAY S. STOWELL, M.A.

JOINT AUTHOR OF "THE SUNDAY-SCHOOL AT WORK,"
"THE SUNDAY-SCHOOL TEACHER AND THE
PROGRAM OF JESUS," AND "MAKING
MISSIONS REAL"

NEW YORK AND LONDON  -  MCMXXXIII
HARPER & BROTHERS PUBLISHERS

STORY WORSHIP PROGRAMS
—A—
PRINTED IN THE UNITED STATES OF AMERICA

B-H

TO

# BETTY AND STEWART

AND TO THE GIRLS AND BOYS
WHO SHARED IN THE PROGRAMS
AND WHO LISTENED SO ATTENTIVELY
TO THE STORIES HEREIN CONTAINED

# FOREWORD

The first three chapters of this book present a discussion of the theory and practice of worship in the church school. The rest of the book contains materials of worship which have been arranged for and used in the church school. They are particularly adapted for one-room schools or schools where two or more departments meet together for the worship period. The stories and talks presented should be of equal value, however, to pastors in the preparation of children's sermons and to others who have occasion to speak to children upon religious themes. They are designed to appeal primarily to Juniors and Intermediates.

It is believed that the careful selection and arrangement of the stories for the accomplishment of very definite ends and the grouping of related material about the important festivals and occasions of the year not only make the book unique, but add greatly to its usefulness and value. The fact that these stories have been successfully used is a testimony to their inherent interest. However, no stories have been included merely because they were interesting. The educational end to be accomplished has in all cases been the ultimate criterion for selection or rejection.

For convenience the arrangement of materials has been made on the basis of calendar months, enough being included for an entire year. Four or five Sundays is not too long to give to the consideration of a single theme, if a definite impression is to be left upon the lives of the pupils. This plan avoids the scattering of effort through lack of purpose while at the same time the theme changes often enough to avoid monotony. So far as possible stories which embody the idea to be presented have been chosen. The pointing of morals is, therefore, reduced to a minimum.

The author acknowledges with thanks the courteous permission of the editors to use material previously appearing in *The Graded Sunday School Magazine*.

JAY S. STOWELL.

# CONTENTS

## PART I: THE THEORY AND PRACTICE OF WORSHIP IN THE CHURCH SCHOOL

CHAPTER             PAGE

   I    WORSHIP IN THE CHURCH SCHOOL . . . . . 13

  II    WORSHIP IN THE ONE-ROOM SCHOOL . . . . . 20

 III    WORSHIP IN THE DEPARTMENTALIZED SCHOOL . . 29


## PART II: MATERIALS AND PROGRAMS OF WORSHIP

  IV    IDEALS FOR A NEW YEAR OF WORK . . . . . 47

   V    LEARNING TO BE THANKFUL . . . . . . . 59

  VI    THE GIVING LIFE . . . . . . . . . 68

 VII    DOING ONE'S DUTY . . . . . . . . . . 77

VIII    CHRISTIAN PATRIOTISM . . . . . . . . . 83

  IX    WHAT IT MEANS TO BE A CHRISTIAN . . . . 92

   X    THE EASTER MESSAGE . . . . . . . . . 101

  XI    THE CHRISTIAN AT WORK . . . . . . . . 108

 XII    MAKING LIFE COUNT . . . . . . . . . 118

XIII    THE WONDERS OF GOD'S WORLD . . . . . . 127

XIV    OUR GREAT HYMNS . . . . . . . . . . 136

XV    THE BIBLE MEETING THE WORLD'S NEEDS . . . 146

# PART I: THE THEORY AND PRACTICE OF WORSHIP IN THE CHURCH SCHOOL

# STORY-WORSHIP PROGRAMS
## FOR THE
# CHURCH SCHOOL YEAR

## CHAPTER I

### WORSHIP IN THE CHURCH SCHOOL

The adoption and use of graded lessons in the church school has created some problems while it has solved others. Superintendents accustomed to uniform lessons often find themselves at sea when graded lessons are introduced. Graded lessons furnish no common theme upon which the thought of the entire school or department may be centered. It is easy to laugh at the superintendent who objects to graded lessons because they furnish him no opportunity to "sum up the lesson," but his objection is based upon something more fundamental than an egoistic desire to exhibit himself. It grows out of the felt need of some unifying thought or activity, something which shall for the moment at least make the group a real unit.

Of course we cannot return to the system of lesson uniformity in order to solve the problem suggested above, but a part at least of the solution is to be found elsewhere, namely in the service of worship. In a strikingly large proportion of our schools there has been no worship. It is true that hymns have been sung and prayers have been repeated with sincerity and devotion, but it is only recently that any really serious attempt has been made to lead pupils into the experience of worship in the church school and at the same time to train them for the more complete participation in the worship of the church service.

We have to some extent wasted a portion of our already limited time because we had certain habits without an adequate vision of their purpose or their possibilities. Thus we have sung hymns to stir up enthusiasm, to get the pupils into a proper frame of mind to study the lesson, to while away the time until late comers should arrive and for various other reasons. Such purposes are no longer adequate. We are now thinking in terms of worship and the church school is deliberately undertaking the new task of training its pupils to participate intelligently and seriously in common worship.

Thus we find ourselves face to face with two distinct yet related elements in our present situation, namely, a diversified lesson material sometimes perplexing the presiding officer and a fresh vision of the importance of training in worship. Surely this coincidence is significant in that it enables us to perform a hitherto neglected function without the necessity of lengthening our school period and it also provides the unifying element for the departments, which some have felt was endangered by the diversification of lesson material.

Whether the unit for worship shall be the department or two or more departments combined the size and equipment of the school and other local factors will determine. Ordinarily a group larger than a class group is desirable for the most effective common worship. If the department is used as a unit the worship may be carefully graded. Experience has demonstrated, however, that where there is a shortage of room the Junior and Intermediate Departments may be effectively united for the service of worship and in case of necessity even a more comprehensive group may be handled.

In planning the services of worship for a graded school it is obvious that they cannot be based on the lesson themes. It is probably well that this is so for the arguments against any attempt on the part of the superintendent to duplicate the work of the teacher are more than the arguments for it. We do have a very practical basis, however, for arranging the services, namely, the church and calendar year. The beginning of the new year of work, the Thanksgiving period, Christmas, the great birthdays of February, Lent, Easter, the springtime, summer and many other significant developments make our path here relatively clear. In any plan the determining factor will ultimately be the results to be attained in the lives of the pupils, but these results can best be secured when due regard is paid to the great occasions of the year as they come. At best, the plan will be more or less arbitrary, but a larger load can be carried with the expenditure of less energy if we make use of all the currents which are flowing our way.

In preparing the material of this book the author has worked on the assumption that the attitude which is best described as worshipful grows more naturally out of the consideration of the highest Christian ideals than out of any attempt to picture God to the imagination. One of the important elements in all worship is a sense of fellowship with the Divine. In this connection we may possibly learn something from human fellowships. Two individuals commune best when, forgetting themselves, they think together about great themes, or work together in worthy tasks. The consideration of a book, the interpretation of a great picture, or the sharing of a deep experience of life will lead two souls into the most intimate relationships. Such communion is at its best when regularity or irregularity of features, style of dress, and all other individual peculiarities are forgotten, and the individuals are conscious only that they are thinking together upon great subjects. Thus it is that the pupil in the church school comes most naturally into communion with God as he tries to think God's great thoughts concerning life, its obligations, and its meaning.

The creation of the attitude of worship is of course the purpose lying deep in the mind of the leader as he plans his service. Curiously enough, however, the purpose of the service may often be best stated in other terms. Real worship, like happiness, friendship and other worth-while things in life, is a by-product. We arrange a service, let us say, with the immediate purpose of making the pupil more self-sacrificing. Through the songs we sing and the prayers we offer and the story which is told we accomplish our immediate aim while at the same time the pupil is led more effectively and more naturally into the experience of worship than would have been the case had there been no immediate purpose to accomplish. The true spirit of worship does not thrive best under the direct attention of the participant. It bears its finest fruitage as a by-product.

In such a service the leader's talk has a distinctive function. It consists in the crystallization of ideals rather than in the impartation of information. It strikes the keynote of the entire service. It must be concrete, adapted to the interests of the pupils and above all deal with a noble theme. Nothing is better than a story or a biographical incident which relates how Christian ideals have been or are being tested and how they stand the test. Object talks are rarely adapted to the particular needs of this type of service; reviews, lesson summaries, drills and similar matters have their place, but it is not here.

It is essential that the worship period of the school be clearly defined and that other items be kept from intruding upon or interrupting it. Announcements, reports, platform instructions and other related matters may follow or be reserved for the closing session of the school, but they should not be included in the brief worship period. To emphasize this distinctive character of the service, the leader may conduct it from behind the reading-desk, and then step from the platform to an entirely new position on the floor before taking up the matters which follow the service of worship.

The limitations of time and the lack on the part of the pupils of the power of sustained attention make it mandatory that the service be brief. It should begin promptly, move steadily and close abruptly. It should not be allowed to shade off into something quite different. The transition to something else should be definitely marked. Every detail of the service must be planned in advance. The slightest indecision on the part of the leader, a delay of thirty seconds from a cause which ought to have been foreseen and eliminated, or any one of many other circumstances which reveal lack of purpose or preparation is fatal.

Throughout most of the service the pupils will be active participants. Only the few moments during which the leader addresses the school are distinctly his own.

The hymn, the responses, the common prayers, the Psalms repeated in unison, all tend to make the service essentially the pupils' service.

If the services are to move smoothly it will be necessary to plan many of them at least one month in advance of the date on which they are to be used. This gives the classes a chance to learn the Psalms and the other common responses as a part of the regular memory work of the school. A Psalm once learned may be used to advantage many times. There should be enough variety in the service to avoid monotony, but too great variety of order and material will detract from, rather than add to the service. Hymns may well be used several Sundays in succession and Psalms and other parts of the service for a month or more.

To make the worship period rich and at the same time brief enough to avoid intrusion upon the other activities of the school is always a problem. There is a constant temptation to lengthen the service. In the long run, however, the best results would seem to be secured from the short service.

The dignity and beauty of the physical surroundings, the nobility of the songs and prayers, the idealism of the leader's thought, all have their part to play in making it easy for the pupil to worship. The most appropriate room available should be used for the worship period. Very frequently this is the church auditorium. There would seem to be many reasons for using this auditorium for the worship of the church school and no very plausible reason against such use.

A school choir to sing the responses and to lead in the singing will add much to the service. Such a choir may easily be secured in almost any school except the very small one. In many schools the organization of several choirs will be helpful. Thus a girls' choir, a boys' choir, and a mixed choir may be used in turn.

In conserving the results of the worship period in the school care should be taken that it may be really a training for a more effective participation in the regular church service of worship and not a permanent substitute for it. In some cases an attempt is made to meet this situation by incorporating the worship of the school in the morning church service. This plan has both advantages and disadvantages. Whatever plan is followed, however, it is of the utmost importance that the pupil trained to worship in the church school early find his way into the common service of worship of the church. Any plan which accomplishes this end is worthy of the most careful consideration.

With this precaution we may give our best efforts to the service of worship assured that we are dealing with an experience which is fundamental in the Christian life and that to train in worship is to fit lives for genuine usefulness. Experience seems to indicate that the period of worship properly conducted may become one of the most potent influences for good which is at present to be found in the church school.

# CHAPTER II

## WORSHIP IN THE ONE-ROOM SCHOOL

Slowly but surely our ideals and methods of church work modify our church architecture. In the meantime, however, our methods of work are directly modified by the sort of building in which we are forced to labor. The number of well-equipped and well-arranged church buildings is steadily increasing but, as yet, many churches are of what may roughly be called the one-room type. A school in such a building may be as carefully graded in its instructional work as a school with a more varied equipment, but it cannot be very thoroughly departmentalized unless various groups meet for the church school work at different hours. This of necessity has a very direct bearing upon any plans for common worship in the church school. All of the members of the one-room school presumably meet at the same time and plans for worship must take into consideration the interests and needs of pupils of all ages. That fact should not, however, lead any worker in a one-room school to abandon all ideal of real worship and to content himself with a mere "opening exercise" in his school. The successful superintendent is not the one who lies down in the face of difficulties, but rather the one who forgets that there are lions in the path and moves straight forward toward his goal. The chances are that he, too, will find that the lions are chained and, therefore, not as dangerous as he had supposed.

It may be granted at the outset that if there are any pupils of kindergarten age in the group they will not be able to enter into the service to any large extent. The presence of very young pupils in the room is usually a problem to be solved and the easiest and probably the best way to solve it is to find some other time or place for their meeting.

To a considerable extent the things which have been said of the beginners are true of the younger primary pupils. They may easily become a disturbing factor in the service and their participation in it is of necessity limited. Experience has demonstrated, however, that primary pupils may be led to participate in many parts of a common service of worship. When this has been accomplished the problem of attention and the consequent disturbance of other worshipers has of course been solved. That the task is an easy one the present writer would not claim, but he does not hesitate to assert that intelligent planning and effort will accomplish wonders even under what seem to be unusual difficulties. There are few experiences more interesting than to watch a group of naturally restive children develop within the space of a few weeks or months habits of attention and joyous participation in worship. The secret lies in a service which is planned carefully, moves steadily, closes abruptly and every element of which is genuinely worth while and to some extent adapted to the comprehension of the group at hand.

This matter of adaptation may seem to be a complicated one when there are so many different ages to consider, but it again is one of the problems which seems more difficult at a distance than when one grapples with it at first hand. The principle is a perfectly simple one, namely, adapt the material not to the primary pupils, nor again to the adults but rather to the older juniors and the younger intermediates. If such a plan is followed it may be assumed that the juniors and intermediates will benefit most by the service. At the same time both the younger pupils and the older members of the school will find in it so much that meets a common need that their attention will be held and their participation secured. It may be argued that such a service is at best a compromise, and that is true. There are hymns, prayers, responses, stories and exercises which would be most appropriate for use with the younger pupils in the group which can be used in a common service only at the risk of losing a vital grip on the older pupils. Older pupils will listen to such elements once or twice out of curiosity, but they cannot enter into them and very soon the entire effect of the service is endangered, if it is planned to meet the needs of the primary pupils. On the other hand if the service is planned for those above the intermediate age, it is doubtful whether the attention of the younger pupils can be permanently held. There is of course the possibility of planning one Sunday for the primary pupils and the next Sunday for an older group, thus endeavoring sooner or later to have a service which is adapted to every group, but this again is bound ultimately to prove fatal. The success of a service of worship depends so much upon the development of habits of attention, participation and response to certain given situations that a service which is constantly changing its character can never be very fruitful as an agency for training in worship. The successful service in a one-room school is one which is planned and carried out by a leader who keeps consistently before him the interests of the intermediates and juniors in the group. It should not be imagined, however, that it is all loss and no gain for the school which is forced to hold a common service, especially if the school is a small one. There is an indefinable something which comes from the mingling of various age groups in a common body which to some extent, although perhaps not entirely, balances the advantages of the school which, because of its size and better equipment, can have a thoroughly departmentalized program of worship.

We have taken so much space to indicate the possibility of worship in a one-room school largely because there are so many such schools. We are well aware that in many such schools there is no effective service of worship, but we are equally certain that there might be such a service if as much attention were given to it as its importance would seem to warrant. The supreme difficulty lies not in the inauspicious circumstances but rather in the lack of vision on the part of the superintendent or other person in charge of the common service of the school. If the manager of a factory is devoting all his energy and that of his organization to the production of Springfield rifles, it is needless to hang around the stock room or the shipping room expecting to see a certain percentage of aeroplanes turned out. If you really want to get aeroplanes from the factory you must first convert the manager to your point of view. If he determines to produce aeroplanes he will introduce new machinery and methods or adapt his old machinery to the new end. There is no hope in the situation until the manager really knows what an aeroplane is and determines that he will bend his energies to their manufacture. The analogy holds good in the church school. The reason we do not have worship in church schools is that we have not paused to consider seriously what worship is, how it might be promoted and what contribution training in worship might make to the lives of our pupils. Our protestations that we cannot have real worship in the average school will have more weight when we have once seriously tried to conduct worship there.

Only recently the writer sat through the "opening exercise" of a large and supposedly well-conducted church school. The session was started somewhat past schedule time, apparently because the leader had numerous matters to attend to just at the last moment. The room was in confusion when he at last took his place on the platform. His first remark was, "Now let's get quiet so that we can begin our Sunday school." The leader of the singing then said, "How many of you boys and girls have song books? Hold them up so that I can see. Well, that's good! Now let us sing number 284—number 284. Has every one found the place? All right now, let us sing." The school then sang the first verse. The leader was not satisfied with the result. He paused before singing the second verse, made some pleasant and witty remarks about the girls outdoing the boys and also about the necessity of smiling instead of looking so solemn. He told a perfectly respectable joke, to which the school superintendent made a witty reply, and the second verse of the hymn was begun. The service was punctuated throughout by sprightly innovations. The pupils were asked to clap their hands during one stanza of a hymn. They responded with enthusiasm and some of the boys even insisted on clapping during a portion of the following stanza, although this did not correspond with instructions received. The prayer was apparently improvised by the leader and while it was a perfectly proper prayer it did not seem to voice the aspirations of boys and girls.

During the prayer one group of intermediate boys, without a teacher, edged toward the door and when they were close enough to it to make their escape assured, they dashed out of the room, leaving the door swinging. At the close of this exercise, which occupied twenty or more minutes of a brief sixty minutes, the classes took up the study of the lesson.

The above case is cited not for the purpose of criticism, for the school in question was above the average in many respects. It was generally well-behaved and well-conducted and the leadership was both intelligent and enthusiastic. The point to be noted is that the leaders were not even attempting to conduct a service of worship, indeed a casual observer would have been perplexed to know just what they were trying to conduct. It is doubtful whether they had any clear idea of the purpose of the "exercise" in which they were engaged. They were evidently carrying out one of those activities which become traditional and which go on and on according to the law of inertia without the necessity of finding a rational ground for their justification.

In contrast to the above was the experiences of visiting a school of practically equal size to the one just mentioned. In this school a definite attempt had been made to develop the idea of worship. The finest room in the building had been chosen for the service. Ushers were at the door and this fact alone gave the pupils a feeling of responsibility and checked before it was born any thought of unseemly exits or meaningless annoyances and interruptions. Late pupils were admitted only at appropriate moments and the mind of the leader was free from all petty matters. At four minutes before the time for opening the service the organist began to play a beautiful and dignified selection. At exactly the appointed hour the school choir of girls sang softly, "The Lord is in his holy temple, let all the earth keep silence before Him." The superintendent rose and said, "The Lord is a great God and a great King above all gods. O come, let us sing unto the Lord. Let us make a joyful noise to the Rock of our salvation. Let us sing together hymn number 64, 'O Worship the King.'" There was no need to ask if every one had a book, for that matter had been attended to by the ushers before the service began, and there was no need to announce the number of the hymn two or three times, for the pupils had been trained to pay attention to the service and one announcement was as effective as three and far more in keeping with the spirit of the service. The entire hymn was sung without interruption; the One Hundredth Psalm was repeated in unison without the aid of books, because the pupils had learned it previously in the classes; another hymn was sung; the pupils were seated, and the leader, in a simple, direct but carefully prepared talk, held up in story form before the vision of the group one of the fundamental attributes of true Christian character. The prayer which followed grew so naturally out of the situation which had been created by the service thus far that it seemed to voice the thoughts and desires of the pupils themselves and as they joined in the Lord's Prayer it was evidently more to them than a mere form. There was an instant of quiet and the school choir sang softly the first verse of "Break Thou the Bread of Life." The moment of hushed silence which followed was an eloquent testimony to the fact that the members of the group had passed through a genuine and uplifting experience in the eighteen minutes since the school had been in session.

The service of worship was over, the leader left the speaker's platform and took his place on the floor. There were announcements to be made and other general matters to be attended to before the lessons of the day were taken up, but they were not sandwiched into elements broken from a service of worship. There will always be many matters of common interest to come before a school which have little or no relation to worship and to try to combine the two is to create a meaningless jumble. Platform instruction and drills are legitimate and useful, new hymns must be learned and memory selections prepared, but these activities can enter into a service of worship only in the most limited way. If the pupil is to enter thoroughly into the spirit of a service of worship he must have it built out of materials which are worshipful, with which he is already familiar and which he can handle with ease. A period may be reserved at the close of the school session for learning new hymns; memory work may be perfected in the class session or in the homes, and hours may be appointed for special training along sundry lines. Thus the necessity for dragging extraneous activities into the service of worship will be obviated.

There is one activity, however, which might well be made a part of the worship period. It is the making of the offering. The difficulty lies in the fact that custom and tradition all suggest a different method of handling the offering in the school. In the Primary and Beginners' Departments it has been made a department function and it has become a real act of worship, as it should be. Among older groups, however, the taking of the offering has developed into a more or less meaningless class function. Our system of reports and often of class rivalries seems to militate against making the offering a genuine act of worship. In many churches the offering has become a real part of the service of worship, a concrete expression of the soul's offering to God. If we were only alert to the lessons which our skilled elementary workers stand ready to teach us concerning the way of handling the offering, and if we had an open mind toward the things already accomplished in the same field in our churches, we might be able to place our Sunday-school offering procedure on a more sensible and pedagogical basis and at the same time further enrich our worship period.

# CHAPTER III

## WORSHIP IN THE DEPARTMENTALIZED SCHOOL

The problems of worship in a thoroughly departmentalized church school are quite different from those in a one-room school. In general we may say that the problems are simpler in the departmentalized school and that the opportunities for worship and for training in worship are better. This is particularly true in cases where the departments are of sufficient size to lend dignity and spirit to the department activities. The service in an extremely small department is likely to suffer at many points, but particularly in the matter of singing. In some cases it will be better to combine two or more departments for the worship period in order to increase the size of the group even though the equipment would warrant a separate assembly. Provided, however, that the departments are of adequate size, a much more comprehensive and satisfactory program of worship can be put into operation here than in the one-room school. The departments represent more or less homogeneous groups and very definite aims can, therefore, be kept in mind in working out the services.

Before determining what those aims shall be, the entire situation must be carefully reviewed. How much do the pupils already know about worship? Are they accustomed to pray at home? At what age are they expected

to begin to attend the regular church service of worship?
Do they actually attend this service? Is there a "children's church"? Do the children come into the regular
church service for the period of worship and for a children's sermon and then pass out? All these and many
more questions must be answered before we can determine what our aim shall be in our program of worship
in the school. Situations are so complex and so individual in character that it is impossible to indicate just what
should be the procedure until all the elements are known.
There are, however, certain principles which may well
guide us along the way.

We may say that the devotional portion of the department program should serve at least three ends. It should
at each age meet the pupils' present needs for a common
service of worship (unless those needs are already met
by some other agency); it should serve as an aid in and
an encouragement to the pupils' private devotions; and
it should serve as a training for more complete participation in the service of worship of the local church of
which the school is a part.

It is evident that we have here a problem which can
never be fully solved until a common program for the
local parish is worked out after the fullest consultation
between pastor, church school workers and parents. Possibly at no point in the entire educational program of the
parish is a complete mutual understanding of more importance. It is perfectly easy for well-intentioned parents, teachers and pastors to work at cross purposes here
and so to accomplish relatively little. In how many par-
ishes, for example, is there any understanding between
parents and teachers as to the proper time for a child to
begin to attend church regularly? Sunday-school super-

intendents waste much good energy urging children to "stay to church" when the child knows full well that it is tacitly understood in the home that he is too young to "stay to church" and that he is not expected to stay. If by chance he did stay, however, he would very often find that his coming was a surprise to the pastor and that not an element in the service had been planned with him in mind. A frank conference (or several of them) between parents, church workers and pastors would soon result in a program which would bring our young people into the church service in groups *to stay,* while to-day an unseemly large proportion of them never become regular church attendants at all. Our failure to do anything like team work here would be enormously amusing if it did not border so closely upon criminal negligence.

At just what age pupils should begin to attend the church service we may not all agree. The present writer, however, is convinced that it should be earlier than we have usually supposed. At any rate *a time* should be set for this step and parents and teachers and pastors should work together to make it an event to be looked forward to and experienced with pleasure. We have a definite scheme for promotion from department to department. Why not include in the plan this still more vital step into the regular church service? It is time to discard the much overworked and threadbare argument so often advanced by parents and, sad to relate, sometimes by teachers that "Children must not be forced to go to church or when they grow up they will rebel and never go to church again." Well, we do not need to "force" them then. Instead let us make church attendance so pleasurable and let us train our pupils so well for participation in the service and let us build up in the minds of our boys and girls and our own minds the assumption that going to church is the expected and the proper thing, that it will be as much taken for granted as the promotion from one department to another. We have talked altogether too much foolishness about Sunday school and church being "too much" for our boys and girls. We do not call five or six hours a day, five days a week, on a hard bench "too much," or, if we do, we still see that our children are on hand for the daily ordeal; we do not call two or three hours in a moving-picture house "too much" for the same young people. No, if we are honest with ourselves, we will be forced to admit that the real reason lies in the fact that we do not consider the matter a vital one and that by our words and actions we have allowed our boys and girls to grow up with the idea that attending church is more or less of a "non-essential industry."

Just how so many parents and teachers got the idea that no pressure should be brought to bear upon children to induce them to attend church is hard to discover, but the fact remains that parents who do not hesitate to bring all sorts of influences to bear upon and influence the conduct of children at every other point, stand altogether neutral when church attendance is mentioned. Only recently the promoter of a junior choir called upon the parents of thirty junior and intermediate boys and girls to consult them in regard to the children's participation in this new venture for the morning church service, a service which incidentally was brief and helpful. In twenty-nine cases the reply was in substance, "I will mention the matter to Johnny, but if he doesn't care to attend church I wouldn't urge him." In one case only did the parent reply, "Johnny will be there." This indifference on the part of parents toward the church service is a great obstacle to progress just at present, but it is no more than the natural fruitage of a system which has allowed a great gulf to become fixed between the Sunday school and the church and which has made no provision for training boys and girls to participate intelligently in the church service.

This entire discussion of church attendance may seem to be apart from our main topic. As a matter of fact it is most vitally related to it. We cannot go far with our plans for worship until it is settled. We must know whether we are expected at a given age to meet fully the pupils' needs in regard to worship, that is, whether our service in the church school is merely a supplement to or a training for the regular church service. In the opinion of the writer, church-school workers should plan to bring the pupils into the church service at approximately eleven or twelve years of age. Previous to that time the matter of church attendance may be left to the discretion of parents. At that time, or what is even more important, at *some time* definitely determined upon it should be taken for granted that the pupils are to become regular church attendants. The period of transition from the Junior to the Intermediate Department would seem to be the appropriate moment for this step. Surely three or four years later is too late to make the transition an effective one. Of course the event must be planned far in advance of every effort made to prepare the pupils for it. It goes without saying that we must also adapt our church service so that our boys and girls will feel at home in it when they arrive. As one means to this end some pastors are organizing large junior choirs so that the young people have a definite part in the service from the very first. If they have been properly trained for this transition the service will not suffer, and, even if a real sacrifice were necessary, the matter is one of so much importance as to warrant vigorous treatment. There is no more vital weakness in our entire local program at present than our failure at the point of transition between school and church. Until we grapple with this problem manfully and fearlessly and in a way in which it has not been handled in the past, our efforts will always move in the realm of relative failure or semi-success.

Having thus gotten in mind some of the fundamental elements in our problem, we are ready to consider a little more in detail the developing purposes which should dominate our work at the various steps of the process.

Ideally the child that comes into the Beginners' Department has already had some religious instruction and has begun to develop habits of prayer. Practically, however, the leader must assume that the pupil knows nothing about God and His care and that the child still has his prayer habits to form. In other words, the leader must begin at the very beginning in her efforts to build up in the child's mind something of a conception of a Father God and his care and to develop the desire on the part of the pupil to talk with this God. Active participation on the part of the pupil is bound to be limited here both because of the pupil's lack of experience and his inability to read. Anything of the nature of a "service of worship" will appear at best only in an embryonic stage. The child in the Beginners' Department accepts God very naturally as a member of the group. His thoughts of God are not limited by the philosophical difficulties which often come later in life. Very naturally God enters into every part of the department activities. The church building itself is to him God's house; the offering is in a very real sense made to God; the songs are sung partly because God likes to hear little children sing, and the prayers are simple talks with God, who is at home, in the church and everywhere and who hears every word that little children say. At no time in the child's entire life is his experience of fellowship with God likely to be more direct and more unrestricted than in these kindergarten years.

The aim of the service at this time should be to meet the child's entire needs for social worship and to stimulate and develop such habits of thought and action as will tend to make prayer natural and easy in the home environment. It is not expected that the child of this age will be found in the church service. The service in his department will be, therefore, in a very real sense his "children's church." The service at this period will meet his present needs, but will only in a general way equip him for further participation in worship. The songs which he sings he will soon outgrow and even the verses and responses which he uses will be forgotten or, if remembered, it will be as the result of accident rather than of design on the part of his teachers. Attitudes and habits will, however, be developed which, if the work of the school is thoroughly coördinated, will be carried over and preserved as he advances to the Primary Department. It is of great importance that the leader of the Beginners' Department understand what is likely to happen in the department to which her pupils are to be promoted, and of equal importance that the superintendent of the Primary Department understand the sort of training which her incoming pupils have had in the Beginners' Department. Only where there is this full and frank understanding between departments can there be such a well-balanced plan as will conserve the interests of the pupil.

In the Primary Department new factors enter into the situation. The fundamental purposes lying back of the services will remain much the same, but the materials out of which the service is built will be somewhat different. In the Primary Department will begin that process of storing away in the mind some of the materials which will be retained and used through life. To be sure, the chief purpose is to provide a satisfaction for the child's present needs for common worship and to encourage his private devotions. Children's songs which will be discarded later may legitimately be used at this time. This does not mean that we can here use songs of questionable theology, of unwise sentimentalism or of markedly inferior poetic or musical quality. Songs which are simple and childish may be used to some extent, however. If purely kindergarten songs are used, the fact that these songs are selected for the benefit of the younger members of the department should be noted and participation in them usually limited to those members. The third year pupils may be requested to serve as listeners or invited to share in the song which is avowedly used for the benefit of the younger members and in which the older pupils share as an act of helpfulness. Thus the spirit of service and the spirit of worship is stimulated by a single act. Distinctly "children's songs" will here be supplemented by some of those simpler hymns which will remain with the child as a permanent acquisition. Their number will not be large, but those which are used can be written on the blackboard, interpreted by the leader and learned by the pupils. In the same way sentence prayers and responses from the Psalms and elsewhere in the Scriptures may be learned and used. The Lord's Prayer and one or two classic children's prayers may be learned and used as common prayers. The Twenty-third Psalm and other appropriate selections may likewise be mastered. An appropriate story designed to emphasize some trait of Christian character and fitting into the spirit of the service may be used, but a distinct line should be drawn between this and such departmental instruction as may be given. The service of worship is not primarily a place for instruction. Although some children will at this age attend church with their parents, it may be assumed that most of them will not do so and that the child's entire experience of worship will be in the department of which he is a member.

With the pupil's promotion to the Junior Department several new elements appear. Up to this time we have been largely content to supply the pupil's present needs for common worship and to promote his personal devotional life. We now undertake more directly that training which will fit him to enter into the service of worship in the local church which he will be expected to attend regularly when he graduates from the Junior Department to the Intermediate Department. We must still meet fully his needs for common worship and endeavor to maintain in coöperation with the parents those conditions which will tend to promote the personal prayer life of the pupil, but we must also take up seriously the further problem of preparing the pupil to share in the common service of the church.

At this stage of the process it is important that there be the fullest understanding between the minister of the church, the chorister and the church school workers if there are to be no fatal slips as the transition is made.

Eternal diligence and careful planning are here as elsewhere the price of success. The service of worship in the
Junior Department must begin to take on something of
the form of the service in the church itself. The pupils
must learn and use some of the hymns, the prayers and
the responses which he will be expected to know how to
use when he enters the church. A conference may reveal
the fact that the service in the church itself is in some
cases altogether too barren and that readjustments will
be needed here as well as in the school. The leader's
talk in the department will fill somewhat the same place
as does the sermon in the church. In most cases this
will be a story or a talk couched in very concrete terms.
In some cases it will be an interpretation of the very
process of worship itself, for there will need to be
much of this if the worship is to be real. Worship is
not an experience to be stumbled into through the use of
certain forms and methods. It is instead more likely to
come as the result of the most detailed planning and the
most sympathetic execution of those plans. Very much
indeed depends upon the spirit of the leader himself. A
leader to whom the service is nothing but a form is not
likely to direct any one else along the pathway of true
worship. It oftentimes seems to be the finishing touches
which really add the most to the effectiveness of the entire service. A brief prayer by the leader growing vitally
out of and immediately following the leader's talk, a response sung softly by the choir, or some other detail may
add the touch which makes the entire service a reality
for the pupil.

At this time perhaps more than at any other conditions
are favorable for storing the mind with choice selections
for present and future use. Entire hymns may be

learned, common prayers mastered and various Psalms and other selections of Scripture committed to memory. Psychologists are not agreed that the memory is actually any better at this period of the child's development than at other periods, but the way does seem to be a little more clear for memory work now than at any time earlier or later in the educational process. Thoroughness is more important than quantity and the selections learned should be used again and again in the service until they have become a part of the pupil's life.

At this time also it is of the utmost importance that the nurture of the pupil's prayer life be thoroughly correlated with the worship of the school. This is important for several reasons. The worship period itself will not be permanently effective unless the pupil learns by experience the meaning of prayer. At the same time the period of worship can do much to make his habit of private prayer a reality. Unless the habit of private prayer becomes fixed during this period it is not likely to be acquired later. Here again, however, teacher, superintendent and parents must coöperate if the best results are to be secured.

The prayers used in the common service of worship and in the class session should be models worthy of imitation. The purpose and meaning of prayer should be sympathetically explained. The Lord's Prayer and other carefully selected prayers should be studied, learned and used. Topics for prayer should be suggested. After careful training along these lines pupils may be led to write out prayers for class or private use, and under some conditions they may be encouraged to offer extemporaneous prayers in the class room. The wise teacher will know when this can be done and when it cannot be done.

The worship program at this period leads out into so many lines that the responsibilities involved become somewhat embarrassing to one who is not willing to labor and sacrifice that the pupil's religious experience shall be broadened. The significant fact that the child is now being prepared definitely for the service of the church itself must be kept in mind. As a part of the preparation for this advanced step it may be well for the entire department to be taken into the church service occasionally at times specially planned and arranged for in conference with the pastor.

Of course if a regular "junior church" is conducted for boys and girls of junior age the whole program of worship in the school must be modified accordingly. The program of worship can then be abbreviated in the school session and the training suggested above can be carried on instead in connection with the junior church. This leaves more time in the school session for platform instruction, drills and similar matters. There is little to be gained and the possibility of definite loss by conducting two duplicating or uncoördinated services in the school and in the junior church.

When the child graduates from the Junior Department we may assume that if our program up to that point has been successfully carried out he is now a regular church attendant. In the Intermediate Department, therefore, we no longer face the problem of supplying the full needs of the pupil for common worship. We can now shorten the service somewhat if necessary, thus giving more time for the class session, or we may begin to develop the initiative of the pupil himself in carrying on the service in the department. We will still continue to use materials which will be used in the church service, but we may begin to sacrifice form and finish to some extent for the purpose of developing initiative on the part of the pupils. The reasons for this are sound. We need in our churches many individuals who can conduct public devotional services of various sorts, but more important than this is the opportunity thus provided the pupils to express their religious aspirations in the presence of their fellows and thus insure for those same aspirations a permanence which they would not otherwise have. It is none too early to begin a process of training which will be continued at least through the Senior Department until the service is placed entirely in the hands of the pupils and carried out according to plans formulated by them in close conference with the teachers and department leaders.

The process of development will be very gradual here. Classes or individuals may take charge of and conduct the responsive services. A group may be made responsible for the selection of the hymns for a given Sunday. Recitations or brief talks carefully prepared may be given by individuals. The common prayers may be chosen and led by others, and in due time members of the department may offer their own prayers. The entire order of service may be planned in advance by a given class and ultimately the entire conduct of the service will be placed in the hands of the pupils. It will require much more skill and effort on the part of the department leaders to make such a program effective than to plan the entire work themselves and conduct the service, but church schools are run for the sake of building up efficient Christian characters rather than for the sake of providing easy jobs for workers. A consistent plan for developing the initiative of the members of our Intermediate and Senior Departments will in six years accomplish much in the building up of strong, self-reliant young Christians. We assume at this time that all the young people in these two departments are attending the regular church service and that it is not necessary to duplicate that particular type of service again in the church school. The habit of private devotions should also have become firmly fixed by this time. We are therefore free to train for leadership as we could not do previously. The service here, while lacking some of the finish of a more formal service, will, in its own way, be just as truly worshipful. It will make a definite contribution both to the *esprit de corps* of the department and to the individual lives of the pupils without attempting to duplicate unnecessarily the form of service held in the church.

There are many questions in regard to worship in the Young People's and Adult Departments which are still unsettled and which can be settled only after all the elements in the local situation are taken into consideration. The existence and program of a young people's society of any sort, apart from the church school proper, the nature and function of the church prayer meeting and many other matters, come up for consideration here. By this time every member of the departments should be tied up definitely to some regular activity of the church. They are no longer in any sense apart from or on probation in the church. It is needless to attempt to duplicate here the functions of the church service. The worship period of the department may become little more than a brief, informal, devotional period with no attempt at a formal service. The distinctive contribution of the church school service of worship has been made during the earlier years and the time can be devoted to other matters.

It will be seen, therefore, that worship in a church school departmentally organized is a matter of rapidly developing importance up to and through the Junior Department. From that time forward some of its functions begin to be taken over by the church service and the service in the school at first begins to change its character and then diminishes in significance as a formal service. It should be noted of course that worship itself is expected to fill an ever larger and larger place in the individual's life as he matures. The changing emphasis grows out of a coördinated program which hands over to the church service itself certain responsibilities as soon as this can safely be done. Thus the time of the school is freed for other matters of importance and a bridge is created which should make it possible for every pupil in the church school to find his way early into the church service itself. When this is accomplished, one of the most fundamental criticisms of the church school will be rendered invalid.

# PART II: MATERIALS AND PROGRAMS OF WORSHIP

# CHAPTER IV

## IDEALS FOR A NEW YEAR OF WORK

### *October: First Sunday*

ORDER OF SERVICE:

I   MUSICAL PRELUDE

II  OPENING SENTENCE: (*Sung or recited in unison while seated*)

"The Lord is in his holy temple: let all the earth keep silence before Him: Amen."

III MOMENT OF SILENCE: (*with heads bowed*)

IV  LORD'S PRAYER: (*or other unison prayer*)

V   THE SHEPHERD'S PSALM: (*Stand and remain standing for the following hymn*)

VI  HYMN: "Rejoice, Ye Pure in Heart" (*appropriate for the entire month*)

VII STORY: (*The purpose of this story is to lead the pupils to appreciate the significance of the year of work just beginning and to undertake it seriously.*)

### THE GREAT STONE FACE [1]

Little Ernest lived in the eastern highlands. At a distance from his home over on the side of the mountain the rocks took on the form of a great stone face. It was a beautiful, kindly and noble face and the children often

[1] Adapted from *The Great Stone Face* by Hawthorne.

paused in their play to look away to it. Sometimes they spoke of the face in hushed and reverent tones as the "Old Man of the Mountains."

In the evening little Ernest would sit by the fire while his father and mother talked of the great stone face and of the legend which had long been related how that some day a man would appear in the valley who would look just like the great stone face. Then little Ernest would sit quietly and wonder when the man would come who would look like the face, and when he climbed into bed it was often to dream of the face and of the man who was destined to look like it.

In the morning Ernest's first thought was of the face, and at night, after his work was done, he would sit in reverent silence by the side of his cabin, looking away in admiration to the face which radiated so much of benevolence and strength.

Each time that a great man came into the valley Ernest hastened to meet him, lest perchance the man who looked like the face should come and go unrecognized and unhonored. Each time Ernest was forced to turn away in disappointment. None of the great men looked like the face.

The years passed and Ernest was no longer "little Ernest." He became "Neighbor Ernest," the man who was the friend of every one and whom every one trusted. The very spirit of the stone face seemed to be working itself out in Ernest's life. Each year found him a little more thoughtful, a little more kindly and a little more unselfish, although sometimes he was a trifle sad because he had begun to fear that he would never live to see the man who looked like the great stone face.

One day, however, good news came to Ernest. There

was to come into the valley a man who was greater than any man who had ever been there before. "Surely," thought Ernest, "this must be the man who looks like the great stone face," and he hastened to see him. But Ernest was doomed again to disappointment; the great man did not look at all like the face.

Quietly and humbly Ernest started homeward; his last hope was gone. No one could come who was greater than the visitor whom they had entertained that day, and yet he bore no resemblance to the face. It was while Ernest was lost in such thoughts as these that almost instinctively he turned to get another view of the face on the mountains which he had come to love. As he turned, the setting sun fell full on his face and the neighbors, who had known him so long, pausing suddenly, discovered that it was Ernest himself who looked like the great stone face. While he had been waiting and wondering when the man would come who would look like the face, he had himself grown into its likeness.

This little story is more than a story for us; it is a parable of what is continually happening in our own lives. We are continually growing into the actual likeness of the things which we think about, live with and admire. Lives are not made strong and beautiful in an instant. It is a slow and steady process. They are built out of individual actions day after day, and the actions in turn grow out of the kind of thoughts which we think and the kind of friends which we have, until we actually come to look like the things and the people with whom we associate.

It is a sobering thought that our very appearance ultimately depends upon the thoughts which we think and the friends which we cultivate, and yet it is an encouraging thought after all. We come to the church school and we study about Jesus and the things which He said, or we learn about Paul or one of the prophets and we go away and it doesn't seem to have made much difference. But we come again next Sunday, and the next, and the next and so on, and finally we discover, or our friends do, that it has made a difference, that we have been building the very best materials into our lives and the very lines in our faces reveal the fact that we have been living in the presence of the best.

It is something like that that our work ought to mean to us this year. At the end of the year we shall be different individuals than we are now, and what that difference shall be the way that we do our work and the spirit which we put into it in the weeks ahead will largely determine.

VIII   HYMN: "The King of Love My Shepherd Is."
IX    PRAYER: *By Pastor.*
X    RESPONSE: (*Sung by school.*)   "Hear us, Heavenly Father, while on Thee we call. May Thy benediction on our spirits fall. Amen."

(*Reports and announcements may be given after this service but not as a part of it.*)

## October: Second Sunday

(*The general order of service suggested above may well be used during the entire month.*)

SUGGESTED HYMN: "Lead On, O King Eternal."
STORY: (*Purpose: To hold up at the very beginning of the year an ideal of Christian courage which will inspire the pupils to more vigorous Christian living.*)

## IRA STRINGHAM, HERO

It was January 8, 1916, Ira Stringham, a sixteen-year-old boy of Jersey City, was on his way homeward. As he was crossing the bridge over the Morris Canal, he saw two small boys break through the ice below. Quickly he ran down the bank of the canal, threw off his coat and shoes, and started out upon the thin and melting ice. He drew his wallet from his pocket and threw it to the crowd on the bank with the words, "If I don't come back, take this to the police."

Carefully he made his way to the hole in the ice and plunged into the icy water. After a bit he reappeared with a boy in each hand. He pushed them onto the ice, only to have it break with their weight. By this time two telephone linemen had arrived. They threw a rope to Stringham. He tied it about the body of a boy and the boy was drawn to safety. Again the rope went out and the second boy was pulled to the shore. The third time the rope was thrown, but Ira Stringham was too far gone with the cold. He tried to speak, but instead he disappeared beneath the ice.

In the pocketbook thrown to the shore was a card of membership in a Christian Endeavor Society. Thus Stringham's identity was quickly established. It was found that he was a poor boy, that his father was dead, and that he had been obliged to leave school to support a mother and a younger brother and sister.

In spite of these unusual responsibilities, Ira Stringham had not missed a session of his Sunday school in more than six years. He was one of the most earnest workers of his young people's society, and he was active in two movements for community betterment outside of the church. At his place of employment he was quiet and unassuming, but a task given to him was sure to be done conscientiously and thoroughly.

He died bravely and nobly, but the reason that he died thus was that he had learned to live bravely and nobly. Ira Stringham, a twentieth-century boy, had in him the stuff of which Christian heroes are made. (Adapted from the *Christian Endeavor World.*)

## October: Third Sunday

SUGGESTED HYMN: "Fight the Good Fight."

STORY: (*Purpose: To hold up at the beginning of the year an ideal of integrity, which will inspire the pupils to renewed zeal for honesty and trustworthiness in daily living.*)

### AN HONEST MAN

Nothing is more characteristically Christian than perfect honesty. It is easy to be honest when there is nothing at stake; but there come times when it costs to be honest. Such an occasion came to David Livingstone.

When David Livingstone went to Africa as a missionary he was deeply impressed with the horrors of the slave trade, and he desired to do something to break it up. He had made his way up into the heart of Africa, and he felt that, if he could open a way to the west coast, it would be a step toward the accomplishment of his desire. To take a journey of fifteen hundred miles through the wilderness was not an easy task, and, unaided, it was an impossibility. He must have the help of the natives.

One of the chiefs would provide the men, if he could be assured of their return. Livingstone promised to guide them on the return journey if they would go with him. Accordingly the party was organized and the journey begun. There were jungles to be penetrated, swamps to be traversed, large streams to be crossed, fierce native tribes to be met, and other dangers of the jungles to be encountered. Livingstone was taken down with the fever and his followers were obliged to carry him on their shoulders. After more than six months of exhausting struggle the weary and distressed party reached the ocean. Here at the coast were food, shelter, medical care, and, above all, a boat just ready to sail for England. The captain urged Livingstone to return to England. Livingstone had not heard from his family in nearly two years; he was sick, but he had given his word to his black companions.

He bade farewell to the departing boat, rested for a time, and then began the severe return journey with his friends of the wilderness to whom he had pledged his word of honor which could not be broken.

We are not surprised to know that when Livingstone finally died, his followers carried his body other weary miles to the east coast of Africa, that it might rest in the land from which he had come to them.

Recently a traveler asked the keeper at Westminster Abbey, the place where England's noblemen are buried, "Which grave has had the most visitors during the past year?" "Without question," replied the keeper, "the grave of David Livingstone." And that was the grave of the man who kept his word when it cost something.

*October: Fourth Sunday*

SUGGESTED HYMN: "O Master, Let Me Walk with
    Thee."

STORY: *(Purpose: To encourage the habit of kindliness
    and thoughtfulness.)*

#### "YOU CALLED ME BROTHER"

Some people are unkind because they are selfish, some
because they are ignorant, and others because they are
thoughtless and lack imagination. Jesus was always interested in people. Little children, the beggar, the sick
man, the woman at the well, all found a friend in Him.
It is always refreshing to meet one who has caught this
kindly spirit of Jesus.

Recently died a man known as the "Sky Pilot of the
Lumber Jacks." Thousands all over this country heard
him speak, saw his genial smile, and felt his cordial hand-
clasp. He gave his life to preaching the gospel to the
men in the lumber camps and to organizing work for
their welfare. Frank Higgins loved men, no matter how
rough or uncouth their exterior might be. So big and
ruddy looking was Mr. Higgins that few realized how
literally he was laying down his life for others. The
dread disease which carried him away was working at
the very place where the strap of his pack basket, loaded
with reading matter for the men, had burned itself into
his body.

On what proved to be Higgins' last speaking trip he
had become so weakened that it was necessary to call
the assistance of a porter.

"I'll have to lean on you, too, brother," said Higgins,

as the colored man took his grip, "for I'm nearly all in," and he placed his arm across the porter's shoulders.

At the train Higgins took out his pocketbook and offered a coin.

"I couldn't take your money, mister," said the porter; "no, sir, I just couldn't."

"Why not?" asked Higgins.

"Why, mister, you called me brother, an' you asked 'bout my wife an' children an' mother. I just couldn't take your money."

It was this kind of love for men because they were men that won Higgins's way to the hearts of those among whom he worked.

One lumber jack whom Higgins had helped to a better life said: "I would lay down my life for Frank Higgins. I love that man."    (Adapted from the *Continent.*)


## October: Fifth Sunday

SUGGESTED HYMN: "We've a Story to Tell to the Nations."

STORY: *(Purpose: To arouse in the pupils a desire for lives of unselfish service.)*


### SERVING TO THE UTTERMOST

Arthur Jackson was one of those big enthusiastic young fellows whom every one is bound to love. There wasn't a lazy bone in his body. At Cambridge University he had been one of the crack oarsmen on the university crew. When his medical course was completed he sailed for northern China as a medical missionary. Here we find him at Mukden in the southern province of Manchuria, January 12, 1911.

Arthur Jackson had only been in China four months, but they had not been idle ones. Measles, mumps, or fever are the same in China as in England or America so that a medical missionary does not have to wait a year or two years as do many other missionaries before they begin their real work. Every day Jackson had been making trips to sick people, performing operations, coaching his Chinese students in football and studying the Chinese language.

On the night of January 12 he was in his room writing to his sister. The bitter cold of the Manchurian winter made the air of his room cold and frosty and occasionally he would rise to walk back and forth or to beat his muscular arms about his great chest. As soon as his hands were warm he went back to his writing. "Whoever invented Chinese," he was saying, "seems to have had an enormous stock of h's, s's, c's, n's, and w's which he no doubt bought at some jumble sale, and it is a wonder that the whole thing has not been sold long ago at another. I can tell you that saying 'Peter Piper,' etc., or any such catch is child's play to managing your s's and w's in Chinese."

For a moment he hesitated, then he plunged again into his letter-writing.

"You may have seen," he wrote, "that the plague is pretty bad in northern Manchuria. We are doing all we can to prevent its coming south. You remember that Mukden is at the junction of the Japanese line running south and the Chinese Imperial Railway running west to Tiensin and Peking. It is an important place as you can see from this sketch." Here he drew a little map.

"Just at this time of the year there are great crowds

of coolies going from their work in the north down into Peking. I am going to examine the passengers to prevent the plague from getting into China. You need not mention this new job I have got to mother, as it would only make her unnecessarily anxious. Of course plague is a nasty thing, but we are hopeful of getting it under now."

Young Jackson rose and paced slowly back and forth in his room. He well knew that in spite of every precaution he might take the dreaded disease, and he knew that, if he did take it, it meant death. A cure had never been known. He looked out of the window on the snowy ground. Away to the west lay the railroad ready to carry its thousands of coolies into China. Who would save Peking and the millions of China? Suddenly Dr. Jackson's shoulders squared themselves. The Master Himself had not saved His own life, why should Arthur Jackson fear to lose his? He walked to the table, sealed his letter and lay down to rest.

The next day his work began. Four hundred coolies were on the first train. Some already had the plague and it was necessary to examine them, separate the infected ones from the rest to die and then take precautionary measure for the others. Dr. Jackson was dressed in white over his fur coat. He wore oilskin boots and gloves, and a shield saturated with disenfectant over his face.

Thus day after day passed for two weeks. On January 23 he lunched with the other missionaries. "Well, we don't make much money out here," he said gayly, "but we do see life." During the twenty-minute lunch he kept them all laughing. He denied that he was tired and then he hastened back to his work. He was in high spirits. The worst seemed to be over and he had stayed by the job and had made good. He went to bed that night, but the next morning he could not rise. In saving others he had taken the plague. Some hours of terrible suffering passed and Dr. Jackson was taken out and buried under the Manchurian snow.

All over China the news of Dr. Jackson's death was carried. Chinese officials of every rank did honor to the memory of the man who had laid down his life for China. It stirred certain wealthy Chinamen as nothing had ever done before. One man sent $12,000 and later $5,000. Others opened their pocketbooks and a great medical college was established in China and named in honor of the man who counted not his life dear unto himself, but who gave it freely for others, and they a people of a different race and a different language.

# CHAPTER V

## LEARNING TO BE THANKFUL

### *November: First Sunday*

ORDER OF SERVICE:

I  MUSICAL PRELUDE

II  OPENING SENTENCES: *(Read by the superintendent or repeated by the entire school)*

"The heavens declare the glory of God, and the firmament showeth his handiwork."

"He causeth the grass to grow for the cattle and herb for the service of man."

"It is a good thing to give thanks unto the Lord."

"Oh, that men would praise the Lord for his goodness and for his wonderful works to the children of men."

III  HYMN: "My God, I Thank Thee Who Hast Made" *(school stands and remains standing for the psalm)*

IV  THE ONE HUNDREDTH PSALM: *(in unison)*

V  UNISON PRAYER

VI  STORY: *(The purpose of this story is to encourage the* habit *of gratitude contrasted with occasional thanksgiving.)*

### THE MASTER OF THE HARVEST

The Master of the Harvest walked by the side of his fields in the springtime. There had been no rain and the corn had not come up. A frown was on the face of the Master of the Harvest; grumblings and complaints were on his lips. Surely there would be no harvest.

The little seeds heard the grumblings and said, "How cruel to complain! Are we not ready to do our best when the time comes?"

The wife of the Master of the Harvest spoke cheering words to her husband. Then she went to her Bible and on the fly leaf she wrote a verse.

At last the rain came and the corn sprang up. The Master of the Harvest was satisfied, but he forgot to rejoice and be thankful. His mind was filled with other things.

When the Master's wife asked if the corn was doing well, he answered, "Fairly well," and nothing more. Again the wife opened her book and wrote on the fly leaf.

Very peaceful were the next few weeks. The corn blades shot up, grew tall and strong, and put forth flowers. The ears began to appear.

The Master of the Harvest walked through the fields; he looked at the ears; he saw that they were small, and again he grumbled: "The yield will be less than it ought to be. The harvest will be bad."

The growing plants heard the complaint, and said, "How thankless to complain! Are we not doing our best?" The farmer's wife again spoke cheering words and then went to her Bible and wrote on the fly leaf.

A drought settled over the land and the Master's face grew very dark. He wished for rain. And then the rain came in torrents. Much of the growing corn was forced to bow before the rushing rain, and some of it could not rise again. The Master of the Harvest railed against the rain. He had not wanted so much.

"Why does he always complain?" moaned the corn plants. "Are we not doing our best?" The Master's wife said nothing, but wrote on the fly leaf of her book.

The weeks passed. The time of harvest came and the barns were filled with golden grain.

One day the Master of the Harvest picked up the book in which his wife had written. He found many verses and among others the following:

"Thou visitest the earth and waterest it; Thou greatly enrichest it."

"Thou crownest the year with thy goodness; and thy paths drop fatness."

"He causeth the grass to grow for the cattle and herb for the service of man."

"It is a good thing to give thanks unto the Lord."

"Oh, that men would praise the Lord for his goodness, and for his wonderful works to the children of men!"

As the Master of the Harvest read, shame filled his soul, and in the place of the old heart of discontent and faultfinding a new heart of thankfulness seemed to grow within him. And the Great Lord of all the Harvests looked down and was glad.

(Adapted from "The Master of the Harvest," by Mrs. Alfred Gatty.)

VII  HYMN: "We Plough the Fields and Scatter."

VIII  PRAYER: *(by pastor)*

IX  RESPONSE: *(sung by school)* First stanza of "Dear Lord and Father of Mankind" *(or other response).*

## *November: Second Sunday*

SUGGESTED HYMN: "The King of Love My Shepherd
Is."
*(The preceding order of service may be used
throughout the month.)*

STORY: *(Purpose: To develop the spirit of gratitude
by calling attention to our dependence upon the services of others.)*

### JAMES AND HIS BREAKFAST

James was not a big boy, and his experience with the
world was limited. The day after the cook left for her
vacation James came downstairs to find the breakfast
steaming hot on the table as usual.

"Did you get breakfast alone?" James asked his mother as they sat down to eat.

"No," said his mother thoughtfully; "I had help; in
fact, a great deal of help; more, I suppose, than you
would ever imagine."

James didn't know quite what his mother was getting
at. At first he thought she was joking, but as he looked
at her face he saw that she was serious.

"What do you mean?" he said. "You don't really
mean that you had so much help?"

"Yes," replied his mother, "that's just what I mean."

Then she began to explain. "Do you see the steaming cup of coffee which your father has? I took the
coffee from the can and put the water on it to boil, but
that was the easiest part of the whole process. Many
months ago, in a country far away, men whom you and
I have never seen planted the coffee and tended it through
the long months of growth. The coffee berries were

picked and dried, put into sacks and carted away to the train or to the ship docks. Here the coffee was stored away and brought to the United States. Once more it was unloaded, and handled again, and again, and again, as it passed through the hands of wholesalers, roasters, and retailer.

"The grocery boy brought the coffee to the door, but his work, as well as the work of countless others who had handled the coffee sacks with aching backs, would have been of no avail without the help of the coal stokers, the sailors, the captain, the engineers, the train dispatchers, the trainmen, and others. Back of them still were the coal miners, the ship builders, and the railroad builders. If any one of them had failed to do his part I could not have finished the job of preparing the coffee."

By this time James was beginning to understand. When he had heard about the throng of workmen who had been engaged in preparing and bringing the sugar which filled the bowl, when he had thought about the complicated process by which the wheat for the bread, the salt for his egg, and the prepared breakfast food which he liked so well had come to him, he began to be filled with amazement. There still remained the dishes, the knife and fork, the table cloth, the table, the stove, the fuel, and many other things, to be explained. It was clear that more people had been at work at his breakfast than he could enumerate.

Never had he thought of the draymen, the laborers on the street and in the factories, the miners in the mines, and the farmers in the fields as working for him. Now he understood, and his heart was filled with gratitude. It made him feel that he wanted to do something useful in the world to pay back a part of what others were doing for him.

## November: Third Sunday

SUGGESTED HYMN: "We Plough the Fields and Scatter."
STORY: *(Designed to make the pupils more thankful for the common blessings.)*

### A LOAF OF BREAD

To-day I want to tell you how one small girl discovered in a very simple way that even the ordinary things which we consume and use from day to day are after all the direct gifts of a wise and benevolent Providence.

A little girl went to her mother one day and said, "Mother, I want to make a loaf of bread all alone."

"All right," said the wise mother. "If you want to make a loaf of bread all alone, go to the kitchen and get permission from the cook and go to work."

The child made her way to the kitchen and there she told the cook, "I want to begin at the very beginning and make a loaf of bread all alone, and I want you to tell me how."

"Very well," replied the cook, "but if you want to begin at the beginning, you will have to go to the grocer and get the flour, as I do."

The little maid went to the grocer and said, "I want some flour, for I am going to begin at the very beginning and make a loaf of bread all alone."

"I can give you the flour," answered the grocer, "but if you want to begin at the very beginning, you had better see the miller, for I get my flour from him."

By this time the little girl was becoming very thoughtful. She hunted up the miller and to him she said, "I started out to begin at the very beginning and make a loaf of bread all alone, but when I went to my mother she sent me to the cook, the cook sent me to the grocer, and now the grocer has sent me to you. I am glad that I have found you because now I can really begin at the beginning for I know you make the flour here from which our fine bread is made."

"Yes," said the miller, "we do make the flour here but we get the wheat from the farmer and if you really want to begin at the beginning you will have to go and see him."

The little girl was determined that she would not give up her task even though it was proving a longer and harder one than she had anticipated, so she made her way to the farmer, this time confident that she had reached the "beginning" of her loaf of bread.

The farmer was very kind and courteous but he shook his head in a discouraging way. "Yes," said he, "I plant the seed and tend it and I gather the harvest but the sunshine and the showers and the little germ of life which makes the seed grow all come from God, so I am afraid, my little lady, that you will never be able to begin at the beginning and make a loaf of bread or in fact anything else. Back of our food, our clothing, the lumber in our houses, the coal in our furnaces and all the other things which we use and enjoy is God. We cannot do even the simplest thing such as to make a loaf of bread without his help."

The little girl had not yet got started on her loaf of bread, but she had done an even more important thing; she had discovered a great truth.

*November: Fourth Sunday*

SUGGESTED HYMN: "Praise the Lord; Ye Heavens Adore Him."

STORY: *(True thanksgiving grows out of contentment. The purpose of this story is to make the pupils contented with the circumstances in which God had placed them.)*

### HOFUS, THE STONE-CUTTER

Hofus was a poor stone-cutter in Japan. His food was coarse, and his clothing was plain, but he was happy and content with his lot, until one day he took a load of stone to the house of a rich man. When Hofus saw the evidences of wealth, he cried, "Oh, that Hofus were rich!"

As Hofus said this a fairy cried, "Have thy wish!" and immediately Hofus was rich. He ceased to work and lived in luxury and contentment, until one day he saw a prince with a snow-white carriage, snow-white horses, a golden umbrella, and many, many servants.

Then cried Hofus, "Oh, that Hofus were a prince!" No sooner had Hofus uttered his wish than he became a prince. Hofus was happy and content as a prince, until one day, riding in his beautiful carriage under his golden umbrella, he sweltered and burned in the rays of the sun.

"The sun is greater than I," cried Hofus. "Oh, that Hofus were the sun!" Immediately Hofus became the sun, and he was happy and content, until a great cloud came and entirely hid the sun.

Then cried Hofus, "The cloud is greater than I. Oh, that Hofus were the cloud!" Immediately Hofus became a cloud. Hofus was happy and content as a cloud, until the cloud fell as rain and swept everything before it except a great rock which stood unmoved by the torrent.

Then cried Hofus, "The rock is greater than I. Oh, that Hofus were only a rock!" Immediately Hofus became a rock, and he was happy and content as a rock, until one day a stone-cutter came to the rock and began to split it.

Then cried Hofus, "The stone-cutter is greater than I. Oh, that Hofus were a stone-cutter!" Immediately Hofus became a stone-cutter, as he had been before, and this time Hofus was really happy and content, for he had learned that there are disadvantages in every station in life, and that the best place for each of us is exactly where God has put us.

(Adapted from a Japanese legend.)

# CHAPTER VI

## THE GIVING LIFE

### December: First Sunday

ORDER OF SERVICE:

I   MUSICAL PRELUDE
II  HYMN: "Hail to the Brightness of Zion's Glad
        Morning."
III THE BEATITUDES  *(Repeated in unison)*
IV  PRAYER
V   HYMN: "Christ for the World We Sing"
VI  STORY:  *(The purpose of this story is to encourage
        the "giving" instead of the "getting" ideal
        of life.)*

### THE MEANING OF SUCCESS

Some years ago there died in the city of New York
one of our earliest and most famous millionaires. He
had begun his life as a poor boy and had become very
wealthy. While he lived he was held up as an example
of success, and schoolboys were stimulated to hope big
things because of his achievements. When he died a
leading New York newspaper said in an editorial: "Not
a single human interest has suffered in the least by the
death of Mr. ——."

This man had made his money by artificially depress-
ing the stock of certain great properties and then buying

while cheap and holding or selling at a profit. His work had not helped to build up industry or to meet the needs of men. His profits had always meant the loss of some one else. His money he had kept for himself and his family. When he died a daily newspaper awoke to the fact that the life of this man who had been rated a success had proved a miserable failure.

Across the Atlantic ocean there lived another man. He never succeeded in accumulating money or other possessions. In fact, he could hardly get enough for the necessities of life. Many times he was in the most distressing situations for lack of money. His clothing was threadbare; his food was inadequate. His life had seemed to be one long series of failures. He saw his plans collapse one after another; his friends spoke of him in pitying tones; other people rated him as a failure. Finally he died a broken-down and discouraged old man.

Not long after his death, however, his grateful countrymen erected a monument in his honor, and they put upon it words something like these: "Savior of the poor, father of the fatherless, educator of humanity; man, Christian, citizen; all for others, nothing for himself; peace to his ashes; to our beloved Father Pestalozzi." This man who had never been able to accumulate much of this world's goods had succeeded because he had been able to give much to the world.

One man failed, not because he was rich, but because he led the selfish "getting" life. The other man succeeded, not because he was poor, but because he led the unselfish "giving" life. Each demonstrated in his own way the truth of Jesus's words when he said, "It is more blessed to give than to receive."

VII PRAYER: *(by pastor or superintendent)*
VIII RESPONSE: *(by the school)*
      "Hear us, Heavenly Father" *(or other response).*
  IX HYMN: "It Came Upon the Midnight Clear."

## December: Second Sunday

SUGGESTED HYMN: "Joy to the World."
STORY: *(Purpose: To encourage the habit of kindliness.)*

### A FOLLOWER OF JESUS

A train was pulling into the depot. On the platform stood a very small, crippled fruit boy. His basket was filled with fruit and nuts ready to sell to the passengers. The train had not yet come to a full stop when a business man had swung himself from the train and in his haste collided with the boy on the platform. The basket was overturned and its contents scattered.

The man saw what had happened, but, as a crippled fruit boy was the only one concerned and as the man was in a hurry, he walked away toward the city without a word.

Just then the train stopped and a traveling man alighted. He, too, had important business in the city, but here was a boy in trouble. The traveling man comprehended the situation in a glance—the scattered fruit, the crippled boy, the distress on his face, and the tears in his eyes.

The man said nothing, but he set down his bag, and quietly, but rapidly, he assisted the boy to gather and replace in the basket the fruit and packages which could be rescued from amid the hurrying feet. The task was completed and the traveler was about to leave when he reached into his pocket and, taking out a silver dollar, he placed it on top of the basket.

As he did so the boy looked up through his tears into the face of the man and said, "Say, mister, be you Jesus?"

"No," said the man, "I am not Jesus, but I am one of his followers, and, as I go about, I try to do the things which I think he would do if he were here."

## December: Third Sunday

SUGGESTED HYMN: "Silent Night! Holy Night!"

STORY: *(Purpose: To lead the pupils to think of kindliness to others as a service to Jesus.)*

### RACHEL AND DAVID

The following is an adaptation of an old legend, but, like all worth-while legends, it contains more of truth than of fiction:

In a place far away there lived a long time ago two little children, Rachel and David. They lived in the country and they were very poor. Their food was coarse, and their clothing was worn; but they were happy and content, for their home was a home where love dwelt.

One cold winter evening as the family was gathered about the rough board table for the evening meal of coarse bread a sound was heard without. Rachel and David listened and then hastened to the door and peered out into the darkness. There in the snow was a little child. "I am hungry and very cold," said the child.

Quickly they brought the little child within. They

placed him by the fire to warm himself and then they shared with him their scanty evening loaf.

Should they keep him all night? There was no extra bed.

"Yes," said the children, "he can have our bed." And so they tucked the little stranger away in bed and then they lay down on the hearth to sleep.

They did not know how long they had slept when they were awakened by the most wonderful music which they had ever heard. It seemed to be without and within and everywhere. They sat up and listened. Then they looked toward the bed where the little child was sleeping. They were amazed to see that his garments were of spotless white and that about his head was a circle of wonderful light.

Then they knew that in taking the little stranger into their home, in sharing with him their fire, their food, and their bed, they had really been ministering unto the Christ Child.

Then, also, Rachel and David remembered the words which they had read in the Book: "Inasmuch as ye have done it unto one of the least of these my brethren, ye have done it unto me."

### December: Fourth Sunday

SUGGESTED HYMN: "Hark! The Herald Angels Sing."
STORY: *(Purpose: To deepen the appreciation of this wonderful story, "which never grows old.")*

#### THE CHRIST-CHILD

Now it came to pass in those days, there went out a decree from Cæsar Augustus, that all the world should be enrolled. . . . And all went to enroll themselves,

every one to his own city. And Joseph also went up
from Galilee, out of the city of Nazareth, into Judea,
to the city of David, which is called Bethlehem, because
he was of the house and family of David; to enroll
himself with Mary, who was betrothed to him. . . .
And it came to pass, while they were there, the days
were fulfilled that she should be delivered. And she
brought forth her first-born son; and she wrapped him
in swaddling clothes and laid him in a manger, because
there was no room for them in the inn.

And there were shepherds in the same country abid-
ing in the field, and keeping watch by night over their
flock. And an angel of the Lord stood by them, and
the glory of the Lord shone round about them; and
they were sore afraid. And the angel said unto them,
"Be not afraid, for behold, I bring you good tidings
of great joy which shall be to all the people; for there
is born to you this day in the city of David a Savior,
who is Christ the Lord. And this is the sign unto you:
Ye shall find a babe wrapped in swaddling clothes, and
lying in a manger." And suddenly there was with the
angel a multitude of the heavenly host praising God,
and saying,

> "Glory to God in the highest,
> And on earth peace among men in whom
>     he is well pleased."

And it came to pass, when the angels went away from
them into heaven, the shepherds said one to another, "Let
us now go even unto Bethlehem, and see this thing that
is come to pass, which the Lord hath made known unto
us." And they came with haste, and found both Mary
and Joseph, and the babe lying in the manger. And when

they saw it, they made known concerning the saying which was spoken to them about this child. And all that heard it wondered at the things which were spoken unto them by the shepherds. But Mary kept all these sayings, pondering them in her heart. And the shepherds returned, glorifying and praising God for all the things that they had heard and seen, even as it was spoken unto them.

## December: Fifth Sunday

SUGGESTED HYMN: "Our God, Our Help."

STORY: *(Purpose: To arouse the desire to make the new year better than anything which has preceded it.)*

### THE NEW YEAR

The passing of the old year and the coming of the new is always an interesting occasion. There is something almost mysterious about the midnight moment which seemes to separate but which really connects the one with the other.

It is wonderful when we pause to think of it how life is measured out to us in terms of new days, new weeks, new months and new years. Each one seems to be a sort of challenge to us to forget the mistakes of the past and to move forward to better things.

If the school record of the past year has been lower than it should have been, the new year offers a chance for us to redeem ourselves.

If our work for our employers has been done indifferently and carelessly, the new year holds out the opportunity for conscientious and faithful service.

If the home life has been soured by our selfishness and

thoughtlessness, the new year bids us make it sweet and clean.

The new year is full of allurements to better things along many lines.

Just what the year, which is about to begin, may have in store for us we do not know; God does not permit us to see the end from the beginning.

Our duty is not to worry about the future, but to do the thing which lies just before us and do it so well that we shall be ready with a clear conscience for whatever may follow.

We stand at the beginning of the year in somewhat the same position as did Christian in Bunyan's *Pilgrim's Progress*. He was anxious to know the way, so he consulted Evangelist.

"Do you see yonder wicket gate?" said Evangelist.

Christian strained his eyes to look, but was forced to reply, "No, I see nothing."

"Do you see yonder shining light?" said Evangelist.

Again Christian gazed intently forward, "Yes, I think I do."

"Then," said Evangelist, "keep the light in your eye and go up directly thereto; so shalt thou see the gate."

That is a picture of life. We do not have to do the duties of next October now, nor even the duties of February. The only task which faces us is the one immediately before us, and there is always a shining light, even though it be faint, to make that duty clear. As we follow it doing the duties one by one as they come we shall find many wicket gates opening before us.

During the months ahead some of you will be passing from one grade to another, some from grammar school to high school, some from high school to college, and others out into the world of business and labor.

Always there is some new task, some new duty, some new opportunity. The only people who fail are those who through discouragement or too great satisfaction over past achievements cease to strive and lie down to rest when they ought to be straining every fiber to advance.

There is an old legend of a shepherd who one day, working in the field, caught a glimpse through the clouds of the place where at the top of the mountain the gods lived.

"Oh," said the shepherd, "would that I could dwell in the heights with the gods!"

Suiting his action to his wish he left his humble abode and set out for the mountain top. The way was steep and long and many thorns were in the path, but the shepherd overcame all difficulties. At last he stood on the heights and sure enough the gods were there.

The gods commended the shepherd for his efforts, and the shepherd, well pleased with himself and with his achievements, lay down to rest. How long he slept he did not know, but when he wakened he was enveloped in a cold mist. The gods were nowhere to be seen. The shepherd called in vain, but finally for just an instant he caught a glimpse through the mist of the gods on a still loftier peak far away.

The shepherd cried out in grief to think that in spite of his hard climb he was still far from his goal. Then he heard a voice from the cloud say: "Foolish mortal, dost thou not know that he who would dwell in the heights with the gods must not sleep but must forever climb higher and higher?"

This is the challenge of the new year to us!

# CHAPTER VII

## DOING ONE'S DUTY

### *January: First Sunday*

ORDER OF SERVICE:
  I   MUSICAL PRELUDE
 II   OPENING SENTENCES: "For the Lord is a great
         God, and a great King above all gods.  O
         come, let us sing unto the Lord; let us make
         a joyful noise to the rock of our salvation."
III   HYMN: "O Worship the King."
 IV   THE ONE HUNDRED TWENTY-FIRST PSALM: *(re-
         peated in unison)*
  V   HYMN: "O Master, Let Me Walk with Thee."
 VI   STORY

### SERVICE THROUGH THE DAILY TASK

Nothing will more surely make for success during the
coming year than a sense of the importance of the task
at which God has placed us.  A task becomes of supreme
value in itself and a stepping stone to something more
worthy only as we put into its performance our best of
skill and devotion.

In one of our western cities there sat one night, several years ago, a number of telephone girls.  As they
responded to the calls during the busy evening hours or
talked together during the quieter hours it was not apparent that they were very different from each other.

In an instant everything was changed. In passing a window an operator discovered that a fire had broken out in the business section next to the telephone building.

"The whole town's on fire, girls! Run for your lives!" shouted the operator. And the girls did run; deserting their posts, they started pell-mell down the stairs—all except Rose Coppinger.

A moment before Rose had been one of a group. Now she was in a class by herself. Calmly she sat at her post, called up the fire department, and then began summoning aid from the country about.

No one thought of Rose Coppinger until the telephone building was in flames; then some one remembered. Desperate efforts were made, and the operating room was reached. Rose was found unconscious at her post, with the telephone receiver strapped to her ear. Wet blankets and restorative measures saved her life and brought her back to consciousness.

When the fire had finally been brought under control, with a part of the town still unburned, the heroism of the telephone operator began to stand out. A committee of citizens presented the brave girl a generous purse "for heroic services in saving the town from absolute destruction."

Better than any purse to Rose, however, was the consciousness that she had taken her humble task seriously, and that when the test came she had been faithful to duty even at the risk of her own life.

(Adapted from the "Christian Endeavor World.")


VII   PRAYER: *(by pastor or superintendent)*
VIII  RESPONSE: *(by the school or school choir)*

*January: Second Sunday*

SUGGESTED HYMN: "Take My Life, and Let It Be."

### FAITHFUL UNTO DEATH

"Policeman Joseph Mangan, a young man not long on the force, is dying in the hospital at Seventh Avenue and Sixth Street as the result of injuries received while rescuing two small children from the third floor of a burning building early yesterday morning." Thus read the newspaper paragraph. That paragraph did not tell the whole story, however.

Young Mangan was ambitious. He wanted to make a place for himself in the world. He passed the examinations, and at the age of twenty-six was a member of the police force of our greatest city. His record for the short time he was in the service was most excellent. The prospect of a long future of usefulness with a pension upon retirement was before him.

Soon after taking up his work he was serving on night duty. At 2:30 A. M., as he covered his territory, he discovered a building on fire. He turned in an alarm and then hastened to arouse the occupants. The second floor was soon cleared, and Mangan rushed to the third. The fire now was burning fiercely, and Mangan and another policeman who had now arrived were nearly exhausted when the last family was guided to safety down the fire-escape.

Just then a mother began to scream: "My babies! My babies!"

"Why didn't you tell me?" cried Mangan, and darted into the building.

He found little Edward crying in the middle of the bedroom, and rushed with him to the street. Then he hurried back through the smoke for Dorothy. He found her in her crib nearly suffocated.

By this time Mangan himself was almost overcome. He reached the stairway, and there he staggered and fell. Mangan's skull was crushed, but little Dorothy, landing on top of him, was uninjured.

The newspaper paragraph tells the rest of the story.

That sort of devotion to duty we have come to expect on the part of policemen, firemen, and missionaries. Because our work is of a different character we sometimes excuse ourselves with a lower standard. Anything short of service to the uttermost, however, is less than our best. Jesus counted not his life dear unto himself, and, however humble our task may be, we may put into it the same spirit which Jesus put into his life and which Joseph Mangan put into his task.

### January: Third Sunday

SUGGESTED HYMN: "The Son of God Goes Forth to War."

STORY:

#### THE JOY OF DUTY WELL DONE

One bitter cold winter morning the wife of a lighthouse keeper was watching the light while her husband caught an hour of sleep. In the gray dawn she saw a small schooner on the rocks. It had been wrecked by the angry sea. Three sailors were clinging to the rigging. Apparently the rest of the crew had been drowned.

Should the woman waken her husband? If she did she felt sure that he would take his lifeboat and attempt the rescue of the men on the wreck. She doubted if a boat could live in such a sea. Her husband might be drowned. If she waited a little the men would probably succumb to the cold and slip off into the sea, or the wreck itself might be sent to the bottom by some huge wave. She hesitated between her love for her husband and her sense of duty.

The stern habit of fidelity to duty through long years of vigilant service overrode every other consideration. She wakened her husband. He went at once in the life-boat, and finally succeeded in bringing all three of the unfortunate victims of the wreck off alive.

The comfort and pleasure which the memory of that awful morning brought to the husband and wife, it is said, was more than that which any five years of softer delights had ever brought. They had learned the joy of meeting unflinchingly a duty which was hard and relentless, and with such a joy the world has few that can compare.

(Adapted from an article by Charles R. Brown in the *Congregationalist.*)

## January: Fourth Sunday

SUGGESTED HYMN: "Fight the Good Fight."
STORY:

### THE CALL OF DUTY

It would be a mistake to imagine that all of the fine and noble things in life are done in the lime-light. There are thousands of instances of heroic devotion to duty which never come to public notice or receive attention merely by accident. Fortunately, duty well done carries its own reward, even when the devotion is unrecognized by those who are closest at hand. To be loyal for the sake of winning the approval of others is to be disloyal to our best.

Nearly a generation ago in one of our eastern colleges a very promising young man had reached his junior year. He was one of the most brilliant men in the class, and he was a general favorite with his companions. His prospects for the future were bright.

In a twinkling everything was changed. Word came that his father had been stricken with paralysis. There was no one to care for the father and mother, and no one to work the little New England farm except this educated, trained young man.

Putting aside ambition, prospects, chosen profession, and all of the things toward which he had been working, the young man took up his new tasks. He became a farmer and cared tenderly for his father and mother as long as they lived. When they passed away the years had already set their seal upon the fate of this man, now no longer young.

On the same farm to which he was called so long ago the man, now well along in years, still lives. His life has not been all that at one time he expected it would be. There has not been much of romance or glamour about it. He is a lonely old man, but he has experienced the satisfaction of knowing that when the call of duty came he was true even though the cost was great.

It is because there is so much of this sort of Christian heroism in the world that we find it so good a place in which to live.

(Adapted from an article by Howard B. Grose in the *Congregationalist*.)

# CHAPTER VIII

## CHRISTIAN PATRIOTISM

### *February: First Sunday*

During the month of February two occasions of nation-wide significance occur. These are the birthdays of Lincoln and Washington. The month furnishes, therefore, a special opportunity for building up an ideal of manhood and Christian patriotism. To this end we have chosen for consideration in addition to Lincoln and Washington, two famous Americans who, each in his own way, helped to advance the kingdom of God in our land.

ORDER OF SERVICE:

  I  MUSICAL PRELUDE

 II  OPENING SENTENCES:  *(Sung or repeated in unison)*
>"The Lord is in his holy temple. Let all the earth keep silence before him."

III  MOMENT OF SILENCE  *(with bowed heads)*

IV  THE LORD'S PRAYER

 V  HYMN: "My God, I Thank Thee."

VI  STORY:

#### BOOKER T. WASHINGTON

The ability and the opportunity to overcome seemingly insuperable obstacles and to achieve great things from

83

humble beginnings have always been characteristic of American life. Few Americans have achieved more than did Booker T. Washington. Born a slave, this man made his way against personal opposition and difficulties until his personality and his achievements were recognized both in the United States and abroad.

As a boy Booker T. Washington did not have many advantages. In fact, he did not even have a name, but chose one for himself. He got his first lesson in numbers from learning the number "18" on the end of a salt barrel. His desire for learning, however, outran his opportunity, and it was a happy day for him when he heard of Hampton Institute and resolved to go there. Walking, riding, working his way, using a hole under a sidewalk for a lodging place, he at last reached the place of his dreams, only to be confronted with the possibility of rejection. His entrance examination was the sweeping and dusting of a room. He used to say that he swept the room three times and dusted it four times. When his examiner returned to go over the room with her pocket handkerchief, not a particle of dust could be found.

When Washington had completed his course at Hampton he decided to give himself to work for his own race. The method of that service was still undecided. After deliberation he chose not the easy way, but the way what seemed to be right. He was sure that the Negro must be taught to work efficiently with his hands, but that was just the thing the Negro did not care to learn. The Negro wanted an education, not that he might work with his hands, but that he might escape that sort of work. Washington chose the unpopular course because he felt that it was the right course. He determined to establish an industrial training school for the Negro. The beginnings of this school were almost too humble for belief, but the faith of Booker Washington was of the sort which removes mountains and which builds schools out of little or nothing. Slowly, and through much labor and toil, he saw his institution grow into one of the great institutions of our land.

In the list of our great Americans the name of Booker T. Washington will always appear as one whom difficulties could not daunt and who, with opportunities which seemed meager indeed, became the leader, champion and prophet of more than ten million people.

VII   HYMN: "O Beautiful for Spacious Skies."
VIII   PRAYER: *(by superintendent or pastor.)*

## *February: Second Sunday*

SUGGESTED HYMN: "Our God, Our Help in Ages Past."
STORY:

### ABRAHAM LINCOLN

Abraham Lincoln was one of those choice spirits who belong to all ages. The stories connected with his life are many and fascinating and of the sort which never grow old. Nowhere, however, do we see the real Lincoln better than in his trust in and dependence upon God.

During the struggle preceding his election Mr. Lincoln went frequently to his friend, Newton Bateman. On one of these occasions he was much depressed by the fact that many of the best people seemed to be opposed to his election. His feelings were greatly stirred. He walked the floor for some minutes, and then, with a trembling voice and with cheeks wet with tears, he said:

"I know that there is a God and that he hates injustice and slavery. I see the storm coming, and I know that his hand is in it. If he has a place for me—and I think he has—I believe I'm ready. I am nothing, but truth is everything. I know that I am right, because I know that liberty is right, for Christ teaches it. Douglas doesn't care whether slavery is voted up or down, but God cares, and humanity cares, and I care; and with God's help I shall not fail."

It was this consciousness that he was working with God and that God was working with him which made Lincoln such a tower of strength in the face of circumstances of almost inconceivable difficulty. Much has been written about Lincoln, the rail splitter, the farm hand, the store clerk, the postmaster, the stump speaker, the story teller and the statesmen. We know of his humor, his wisdom and his unfailing honesty. It will do us good occasionally to get back of all of these and to think of Lincoln as the reverent man who believed so firmly and depended so constantly upon God.

It was upon such a faith that his reverence for the common people and for the laws of both God and man was founded. With such a background it was natural for him to say:

"Let reverence for the laws be breathed by every American mother to the lisping babe that prattles on her lap; let it be taught in schools, in seminaries and in colleges; let it be written in primers, spelling books and in almanacs; let it be preached from the pulpit, proclaimed in legislative halls and enforced in courts of justice. And, in short, let it become the political religion of the nation; and let the old and the young, the rich and the poor, the grave and the gay of all sexes and tongues and colors and conditions sacrifice unceasingly upon its altars."

Upon the death of Lincoln, Henry Ward Beecher said:

"Again a great leader of the people has passed through toil, sorrow, battle and war, and has come near to the promised land of peace into which he might not pass over. Who shall recount our martyr's sufferings for this people? By day and by night he trod a way of danger and of darkness. On his shoulders rested a government which was dearer to him than his very life. Upon thousands of hearts great sorrows and anxieties have rested, but not on one such and in such measure as on that simple, truthful, noble soul, our sainted and beloved Lincoln.

"Never impassioned, nor yet despondent, he held on through four dreadful, purgatorial years wherein God was cleansing the sin of his people as by fire."

Such was the man whose memory we honor at all times, but particularly on his birthday.

*February: Third Sunday*

SUGGESTED HYMN: "America."
STORY:

### GEORGE WASHINGTON

In the year 1745 a thirteen-year-old boy in the new country of America wrote for his own personal guidance the following: "To labor to keep alive in my breast that little spark of celestial fire called conscience." Few individuals ever succeeded better in carrying out such a purpose than did this boy, George Washington. In personal relations, in business, in public life, Washington's fidelity to the inner voice was his outstanding characteristic.  The business transactions conducted by Washington were many and of great variety, yet it is said that there is not a case on record "of any attempt on his part to get the better of any of his fellows."  The product of his estate were passed without inspection, so well known was his fidelity to truth and honesty.  The inner voice which Washington followed was more to him than a mere mechanism for warning him of the wrong path.  God was real and personal to him.  In all of the crises of life, Washington's faith in a God of love stood by him.  Without such faith he could not have borne the burdens which were his.

During the terrible winter at Valley Forge, Mr. Isaac Potts was one day walking over his estate when, in the woods by the side of a stream he heard a very solemn voice.  He approached the spot, and there discovered Washington's horse tied to a tree.  At a little distance in a thicket he saw Washington on his knees in the snow in prayer.  Reverently Mr. Potts turned away, and as he returned to the house he burst into tears, saying to his wife, "If there is any one on this earth that the Lord will listen to, it is George Washington."

This fine faith of Washington's was the direct result of the training which he had received from his mother.  The story of his relations with his mother is a beautiful one.  One incident is typical.

One day in the year 1789 word arrived at Mount Vernon that Washington had been unanimously elected the first President of the United States, and his presence was urgently requested at the seat of government.  Hastily Washington put his own affairs in order and then, just at nightfall, mounting his fleetest horse, he set out, not for the seat of government but to say good-by to his aged mother. All through the hours of the night he rode and the next morning appeared unannounced at his mother's door. A brief visit and loving farewell, and Washington was on his way back to Mount Vernon. By nightfall he was again at home, having at the age of fifty-seven ridden more than eighty miles in twenty-four hours, over roads that were rough and primitive, for the sake of a last farewell with the mother to whom he owed so much. The next morning he was ready to start on his journey of two hundred and fifty miles to New York City.

We may well be thankful that in the most difficult moments in the history of our country we have had in the presidential chair men who believed in God and prayed to Him—Washington and Lincoln were men who under the most trying circumstances have kept their faith in the outcome of events clear and strong because they believed in God and carried their burdens to Him in prayer. We, who are citizens of the United States, may well try a little harder than ever before this year to be true to the high ideals set and the trust left to us by such leaders.

## February: Fourth Sunday

Suggested Hymn: "O Beautiful for Spacious Skies."
Story:

### JACOB A. RIIS

The acts of children are frequently the prophecies of the future. This was true at least in the case of one of our noted Americans who died a few years ago. At the age of twelve years, Jacob A. Riis, then a boy in Denmark, offered the money which had been given him for Christmas to a dweller in a slovenly tenement on condition that he would clean up his house and his children,

No one realized then that Jacob would become an international character famed for his work in improving the condition of tenement dwellers.

Jacob Riis learned the carpenter trade, and at eighteen he asked the girl of his dreams to become his wife. She refused, and Denmark no longer had any attractions for Jacob. He wanted to get as far away as possible, and he started for America.

The experiences which Jacob had in trying to get established in the new world were severe, but they helped to make him a more useful man later. One night, in desperation, he applied at the police station for lodging. It was an experience never to be forgotten by Riis, for in the morning he saw a policeman, in a fit of rage, dash out the brains of a little dog which had been the wanderer's only friend. With rage such as he had never known, Riis hurled stones at the police station until the policemen drove him away. For years he carried the bitter memory of his unjust treatment in his heart. Many times he thought of vengeance. The years rolled around, and at last the opportunity for revenge came. He faced it squarely and turned from it. He would not seek personal satisfaction, but he would destroy the entire system of filthy and corrupt police lodging-houses in New York.' Progress was slow, but after many years Mr. Riis saw the last police lodging-house closed.

This, however, was only an incident in a much larger work. Gradually Mr. Riis came to give his entire time to the work of improving slum conditions. The famous Mulberry Bend, with its filth, its crime, its squalor, was forced to give way before his work, and a beautiful park took its place. He took upon himself the task of bringing cheer into thousands of homes which were cheerless and of making living conditions more bearable for those who were ground under the heel of poverty. His books, "How the Other Half Lives," "The Battle with the Slums," "The Children of the Tenements," and others, have done more than perhaps any other books toward improving the condition of the poor in the cities of the United States.

In the midst of conditions which were disheartening in the extreme, Jacob A. Riis was able to maintain his optimism. The following words near the close of his life are typical of the man: "I have lived in the best of times. I have been very happy. No man ever had so good a time." By the pathway of service to his fellows the little Danish boy had become the famous American to whom Presidents of our republic were proud to do honor.

# CHAPTER IX

## WHAT IT MEANS TO BE A CHRISTIAN

### *March: First Sunday*

This is the season of the year when many Sunday-school pupils are looking forward to joining the church. Themes which have to do with what it means to be a Christian will therefore be appropriate for the worship period.

ORDER OF SERVICE:

I  MUSICAL PRELUDE:

II  OPENING SENTENCES *(by leader or entire school)*
> "I will praise the Lord at all times: His praise shall continually be in my mouth; O magnify the Lord with me, and let us exalt His name together."

III  THE ONE HUNDREDTH PSALM: *(repeated in unison; school seated)*

IV  HYMN: "God is Love" *(school standing)*

V  STORY: *(This talk is designed to make the pupils realize that the Christian life is always a purposeful life.)*

### DERELICTS AND OCEAN LINERS

Out on the Atlantic Ocean there are two kinds of boats. There is the great ocean liner with its chart, its compass, its pilot, and its crew. It has its starting place, its definite course, and its destination. It has a purpose. There is another sort of boat, however. It has no chart, no compass, no pilot, no crew, no starting place, no course, no destination and no purpose. It is known as a derelict. It simply drifts. It is of no value to itself, and it is a menace to all who travel the seas. The United States Government is forced to spend thousands of dollars each year for the destruction of derelicts.

These two kinds of boats typify two kinds of lives. One is dominated by a great purpose, and makes every faculty bend toward the fulfillment of that purpose. The other drifts at the mercy of circumstances. The great religious men have always been men of purpose. We read that "Daniel purposed in his heart," and centuries later we remember Daniel with admiration. Paul was dominated by a great purpose. "This one thing I do," was characteristic of his whole nature. Martin Luther had a great purpose, from the accomplishment of which no danger could deter him.

Christianity comes into a life to give it purpose. It takes lives which would otherwise drift at the mercy of circumstances, and makes them of service to others. There are purposes which dominate lives besides the Christian purpose, such as the purpose to make money for selfish ends or to seek pleasure. All such purposes are more or less unworthy in character. Christianity alone furnishes a great unselfish purpose worthy of a son of God.

Every Sunday-school pupil must decide sooner or later whether he will be a derelict or an ocean liner—the first a menace to itself and to others, and the second a blessing to the world because it has a purpose—and that purpose is to serve.

VI   HYMN: "O Master, Let me Walk with Thee"
        (school standing)
VII  PRAYER: (by leader, or unison prayer)
VIII RESPONSE: "Hear us, Heavenly Father, while on
        Thee we call.  May Thy benediction on our
        spirits fall" (or other appropriate response)

## March: Second Sunday

SUGGESTED HYMN: "Brightly Gleams Our Father's Mercy."

STORY: (Purpose: To make the pupils more helpful to others, by suggesting that helpfulness is characteristic of the Christian.)

### THE HELPFUL HABIT

Jesus could always discover opportunities for helping others.  In fact, that was one of his chief characteristics, as it has been of his closest followers throughout the ages.  The best Christians have been those who carried good cheer and comfort with them as they passed along.

Phillips Brooks walked down the street one morning, and a newspaper man wrote, "The day was dark and rainy, but Phillips Brooks passed down Newspaper Row, and all was bright."

It is said that Henry Ward Beecher was walking one day down the streets of Brooklyn when he discovered a small boy sitting on the curb and crying as though his heart would break.  The heart of the man was touched.

He picked the little fellow up in his strong arms and said, "What's the trouble, my little man?"

The boy looked through his tears and replied, "There ain't nothing the trouble, now you've come."

There are many places in the world where trouble could be eliminated if Christians took their task a little more seriously, and went about carrying the encouragement and the good cheer which is the Christian's by right.

Jesus taught that a man succeeds in proportion as he learns to give rather than to get. It is not always an easy lesson to learn.

Whether or not we really live the giving life depends a good deal upon what we are. If we make ourselves strong and joyous and kind, we shall inevitably be giving continually of our strength, our joy, and our kindliness, even when we are least conscious of it. The best things in life we cannot keep to ourselves even if we would. The first step in worth-while giving is to make ourselves worth while.

Over in India there grew on the grounds of a certain prince a mango of marvelous delicacy. Because the fruit was so fine, the prince said, "I will keep this entirely for myself."

In order to carry out his purpose, he built a high wall and placed soldiers about the tree to guard it night and day. Some years ago, however, a strong wind broke one of the branches from the tree, and it fell outside the wall. A pedestrian passing saw the twig in the path, carried it home and then, wrapping it carefully, sent it to a friend in Florida. The Florida friend nursed the little twig with great care; it grew into a tree and just recently it bore its first crop of forty mangoes. It is expected that before long there will be in the United States an entire grove of mango trees of the same remarkable character as the single tree in India, which the prince is guarding so jealously for his own use and which he thinks he has kept entirely to himself.

The best things in life simply insist on being shared with others. It is our business to see that in our own natures we possess the best.

## March: Third Sunday

SUGGESTED HYMN: "Saviour, Like a Shepherd Lead Us."

STORY: *(Purpose: To help the pupils understand the meaning of faith.)*

### A CHILD'S FAITH

One of the things which should characterize a Christian is faith. Nothing can really harm one who trusts himself in the keeping of the God whom Jesus revealed. Sometimes we pray "Thy will be done" as though we were praying for the very worst thing which could possibly happen to us instead of the best.

A small boy had a pet kitten. It became necessary to dispose of the kitten. Ether was administered, and the boy sadly took his pet to the garden for burial.

Some time later the boy was on his way to the doctor's office, where a slight operation was to be performed. The mother explained that it would be necessary for the boy to take ether.

"But, mother," he said, "I don't want to take the ether."

"Mother thinks you had better take it."

"But I don't want to take it," said the boy.

"Mother wants you to," said the mother.

"All right," was the reply, "if you think it best, and you want me to take it, I will."

The two met the doctor. The ether was administered, and the boy was soon safely out from under its effects.

As he recovered consciousness, he looked up into his mother's face and said, "Why mother, I didn't die, and you didn't take me out and bury me like the kitten, did you?"

Then for the first time the mother realized that the boy had consented to take the ether because she thought it was best, when he believed that he would die and be buried as the kitten had been. Because he trusted her implicitly, he had put his life in her keeping.

This faith, so natural to the child, is not always easy to achieve, but it is the kind of trust which those who believe in the great Father-God of Jesus may have.

A Christian may have the faith of Job when he said, "Though He slay me, yet will I trust in Him"; or of Isaiah when he said, "Thou wilt keep him in perfect peace whose mind is stayed on Thee: because he trusteth in Thee."

## March: Fourth Sunday

STORY:   *(Purpose: To help the pupil to feel that in striving for the Christian ideal he may rely upon help from above.)*

### THE MASTER PAINTER

Sometimes young people become discouraged in their attempts to lead the Christian life, because Christian standards are so high, and so difficult to attain. We must remember, however, that when we become Christians we have the finest and strongest forces of the universe working with us.

A painter was trying to copy the masterpiece of his teacher. Day after day, week after week, and month after month he worked. The outlines he could trace, and in many respects he made his painting look like that of his master. But the expressions of the faces and other fine points which made for the perfection of the original he could not reproduce.

At last, one day, tired and discouraged, he laid his head on the table and fell asleep. As he was sleeping the master himself came into the room. He saw what his pupil had been trying to do. He noted the places where he had failed. He saw the brush which had fallen from the hand of the sleeper. Picking up the brush, the master touched the picture here and there until it stood out just like the original. Quietly the master put aside the brush and left the room.

The pupil slept on. Finally he awoke, and looking up at his canvas he discovered that while he had been sleeping the picture had been finished.

It is in some such way, I suppose, that the Christian who does his best to attain the ideal which seems unattainable will find that he has achieved far more than he expected, because the great Master of all lives has been working with him.

### March: Fifth Sunday

SUGGESTED HYMN: "Light of the World, We Hail Thee."

STORY: *(Presenting Christianity as a triumph over death.)*

### TYLTYL AND MYTYL

If you have read the story of "The Bluebird" you will remember that there was once a little boy and a little girl named Tyltyl and Mytyl. One winter's night they were sound asleep when suddenly there appeared a very queer old woman demanding that the children secure for her "the grass that sings" or "the bluebird." The children had neither. The fairy, for such she proved to be, finally admitted that she could get along without the "grass that sings," but insisted that she must have "the bluebird." Accordingly she waved her wand, the old bedroom was transformed, familiar objects took on life and spoke, and the children started out upon their search for "the bluebird," which it is said always bring happiness to the one who possesses it.

In their search the children visit the Kingdoms of the Past, of the Future, and of the Dead, and the Realm of Night. It is while they are in the Kingdom of the Dead that a very interesting and significant incident occurs.

The children come timorously to an old country churchyard, where the moonlight falls on mossy slabs, sunken crosses, and neglected mounds. Little Mytyl is very much afraid, especially because her brother has told her that at the hour of midnight the dead leave their graves.

Mytyl wishes to run away, but Tyltyl, although frightened, insists on staying. At last the clock begins to strike. The children tremble. There is a moment of silence. The crosses totter, the mounds open, the slabs lift. They look for the dead, but no dead appear.

Instead, there arises gradually a blossoming of beautiful white flowers filling and transforming the old cemetery into a fairy garden. Dew sparkles, flowers bloom, wind murmurs in the foliage, bees hum, birds appear and fill the place with their intoxicating song of life and sunshine and joy.

Amazed, the children hold tightly to each other's hands and look timidly among the flowers for some trace of graves, but no graves appear. Mytyl, searching among the grasses, asks, "Where are the Dead?" and Tyltyl, in his childish voice, cries out with all the earnestness born of a new discovery, "There are no dead!"

The children in their innocence had discovered the message which Easter has for you and for me and for all the world this year. It is a message that will bring cheer to millions of aching hearts to-day:

"There are no dead, for Jesus, on that first Easter morning, so long ago, triumphed over death, and henceforth its sting is gone for those who commit themselves to His keeping."

This is the message of Easter to us this Easter time.

# CHAPTER X

## THE EASTER MESSAGE

### *April: First Sunday*

ORDER OF SERVICE:

I MUSICAL PRELUDE

II THE ONE HUNDREDTH PSALM: *(school standing and repeating in unison)*

III HYMN: "We March, We March to Victory."

IV PRAYER OF GOOD WILL: "Our Father in heaven, we thank thee that in work and in play, in joy and in sorrow, thou art the friend and companion of us all. When we do wrong and grieve thee, thou art ready to forgive. When we do right, thou art glad. May no hatred or envy dwell in our hearts. Keep our hands from selfish deeds and our lips from unkind words. Teach us to bring cheer to any who suffer and to share freely with those who are in need. So may we help thee, our Father, to bring peace, good will, and joy to all thy children. Amen."

(This prayer is taken from Hartshorne's *Book of Worship for the Church School.* Published by Charles Scribner's Sons. It is fine enough to be learned by the pupils and adopted as the school prayer.)

V  HYMN: "Rejoice, Ye Pure in Heart."

VI  STORY: *(The purpose of this story is to help the pupil to appreciate the significance of the Easter season and the Easter message.)*

### HE ROSE AGAIN

A gentleman in one of our great cities stood looking at a picture in a store window. It was a picture of the crucifixion of Jesus. Suddenly he became aware that a street boy was standing by his side. "That's Jesus," said the boy. The man made no reply, and the boy continued, "Them's Roman soldiers," and, after a moment, "They killed him."

"Where did you learn that?" said the man.

"In a little mission Sunday school around the corner," was the reply.

The man turned and walked thoughtfully down the street. He had not gone far when he heard a youthful voice crying, "Say, Mister! Say, Mister!"

The gentleman turned to see his friend of the street hurrying toward him.

"Say, Mister," said the boy, "I wanted to tell you that he rose again."

That message, which was nearly forgotten by the boy, is the message which has been coming down through the ages. It is a message of Easter this year and every year, a message of the eternal triumph of life over death, a triumph which is continually being reënacted in the life of the Christian.

Many years ago a European princess died. That her body might never be disturbed, she arranged to have her grave covered with huge blocks of granite securely clamped together. Upon the grave this inscription was placed: "This burial place, purchased to all eternity, must never be opened."

The months and the years passed, and the mandate inscribed in granite was respected. There was every indication that the wish of the dying princess would be carried out, and that her grave would forever remain closed. One day, however, a visitor noticed what seemed like a displacement of one of the large granite blocks. As the days passed this became more pronounced, until at last the granite gave way entirely, and a young oak tree stood forth, opening the grave which was to remain undisturbed through all eternity.

A tiny acorn had fallen all unnoticed into the grave, and what men dared not to do the acorn had done because it had in itself the germ of life. The seed of life, buried in the place of death, had brought forth of its own kind in spite of all efforts to suppress it.

Possibly no better illustration than this could be found of the way the Christian life operates. Christianity is not a set of rules or a cut-and-dried system to which all must conform. Rather, like the acorn, it is the germ of a new life coming to break up old traditions and habits and to remake the life from within.

VII  PRAYER

VIII  RESPONSE: *(by the school; an appropriate verse of a selected hymn sung softly)*

## April: Second Sunday

SUGGESTED HYMN: "Christ the Lord Is Risen To-day."

STORY:

### THE RESURRECTION

Now on the first day of the week cometh Mary Magdalene early, while it was yet dark, unto the tomb, and seeth the stone taken away from the tomb. She runneth therefore, and cometh to Simon Peter, and to the other disciple whom Jesus loved, and saith unto them, They have taken away the Lord out of the tomb, and we know not where they have laid him. Peter therefore went forth, and the other disciple, and they went toward the tomb; and they ran both together: and the other disciple outran Peter, and came first to the tomb; and stooping and looking in, he seeth the linen cloths lying; yet entered he not in. Simon Peter therefore also cometh, following him, and entered into the tomb; and he beholdeth the linen cloths lying, and the napkin, that was upon his head, not lying with the linen cloths, but rolled up in a place by itself. Then entered in therefore the other disciple also, who came first to the tomb, and he saw, and believed. For as yet they knew not the scripture, that he must rise again from the dead. So the disciples went away again unto their own home.

But Mary was standing without at the tomb weeping; so, as she wept, she stooped and looked into the tomb; and she beholdeth two angels in white sitting, one at the head, and one at the feet, where the body of Jesus had lain. And they say unto her, Woman, why weepest thou? She saith unto them, Because they have taken away my Lord, and I know not where they have laid him. When she had thus said, she turned herself back, and beholdeth Jesus standing, and knew not that it was Jesus. Jesus saith unto her, Woman, why weepest thou? whom seekest thou? She, supposing him to be the gardener, saith unto him, Sir, if thou hast borne him hence, tell me where thou hast laid him, and I will take him away. Jesus saith unto her, Mary. She turneth herself, and saith unto him in Hebrew, Rabboni; which

is to say, Teacher.  Jesus saith to her, Touch me not;
for I am not yet ascended unto the Father; but go unto
my brethern, and say to them, I ascend unto my Father
and your Father and my God and your God.

## April: Third Sunday

SUGGESTED HYMN:  "May the Master Count on You?"

STORY:  *(The particular purpose of this story is to
increase the sense of responsibility on the part of
those pupils who have united with the church at
the Easter season.)*

### JESUS' PLAN

Rev. S. D. Gordon, in one of his "Quiet Talks," al-
lows his imagination to picture reverently what might
have occurred when Jesus returned to be with the Father.
It is somewhat as follows:

Gabriel says to Jesus, "So you have been down on
the earth for a long time."

"Yes," replies Jesus.

"And you have lived and suffered and died for the
people," says Gabriel.

"Yes," is the reply.

"And I suppose that every one knows about what you
have done," continues Gabriel.

"No," answers Jesus.

"Well, what arrangements did you make for spreading the news and for carrying on the work which you
have begun?  Have you any plan?" queries Gabriel.

"Yes," replies Jesus; "I gathered a small group of
followers and trained them as best I could.  I lived
with them and worked with them, and now they are

going out to tell others. Those others will tell still others, and so the work will go on until the whole wide world is encompassed."

"But suppose that the little group does not prove faithful," asks Gabriel; "suppose that Peter goes back to his fishing, that John gets discouraged, and that the others give up their work; have you any other plan?"

"No," says Jesus, "I have no other plan. I am depending on them."

This is the message which comes to us at the close of the Easter season. We are the emissaries of Jesus, doing his work and spreading the good news of him. If we fail, the work fails indeed, for he has no other plan. He is depending on us.

## April: Fourth Sunday

SUGGESTED HYMN: "Faith of Our Fathers."

STORY: *(The purpose of this talk is to emphasize the importance of the times of quiet communion with God.)*

### THE MINISTRY OF QUIET

A student of archæology not long ago discovered a very important inscription which had been dimmed by the ages. Naturally he was anxious to determine its meaning and significance, but he did not attempt to read the inscription at the time. Instead, he returned home and rested his eyes three days. At the end of that time he went back and read the inscription. He could not run the risk of reading inaccurately or of missing something in the inscription while his eyes were blurred with many other things.

An acquaintance of an artist was one day invited to

view a great new picture. Upon arrival at the artist's home the man was ushered into a partially darkened room and left alone for some time. He felt that he was not receiving the cordial welcome which he had expected. At last the artist appeared and explained that the quiet of the darkened room was a necessary preliminary in order that his visitor might get the glare of the street out of his eyes. Otherwise much of the beauty of the picture could never have been appreciated.

These two incidents are parables of significance for the Christian. The rush of events in our present-day life tends to make the Christian forget the times for quiet communion with himself and with his God; yet these times are as essential for the building up of strong Christian character as was the three-days' rest to the archæologist or the period in the darkened room to the artist's friend. We must take time regularly from the rush of events if we would "get the glare of the street out of our eyes" and discover some of the deep things of God which have been unappreciated by us. The habit of daily quiet communion with God will place the life of the Christian upon a sure foundation.

# CHAPTER XI

## THE CHRISTIAN AT WORK

### *May: First Sunday*

The general purpose of the work of the month is to lead the pupils to understand that to serve one's fellow-men in need is to serve God. The leader's talk for the second Sunday of the month, however, is prepared especially for Mother's Day.

ORDER OF SERVICE:

I   MUSICAL PRELUDE
II  OPENING SENTENCES: "I will bless the Lord at all times; his praise shall continually be in my mouth. Oh, magnify the Lord with me, and let us exalt his name together."
III HYMN: "When Morning Gilds the Skies."
V   Brief invocation by the leader, followed by the Lord's Prayer.
VI  STORY:

#### "INASMUCH"

Jesus seemed to expect that his followers would go about the world doing some of the same sort of things which he did while he was on earth. Of him it was said, "He went about doing good." He comforted the broken-hearted, he relieved the distressed, he healed the sick, and he carried with him always the spirit of helpfulness and good cheer.

There is an old story of a woman who had heard that Jesus was to visit her town and that he would dine at the house which was best prepared to receive him. The woman determined that her house would be the one chosen by the Master. Accordingly she scrubbed and polished the house throughout and then set about the preparation of a wonderful meal.

Everything went well except that the woman had a number of interruptions as her work progressed. A plainly dressed caller tried to interest her in plans for improving the conditions of the needy in the community, but the woman replied, "I cannot give time to you to-day. The Master may come at any moment, and I must hasten my preparations."

A small boy playing in the street cut his finger and came to the door, asking for a cloth to cover the injured member. "Get away from here quickly," said the woman. "I have no time to hunt cloths to-day, and besides, you are getting blood on my steps."

The pastor called to ask for a few dollars for the needy ones in the foreign-mission field. "I believe in caring for the folks at home first," said the woman; "besides, I am very busy to-day getting ready for the coming of the Master."

There were other interruptions, and the woman at times became irritable. At last, however, the work was done, and she sat down in her spotless house to wait for the Master. All through the late afternoon and on into the night she waited, but the Master did not come.

The next morning, tired and dejected, she went about her daily task. As she worked her eyes fell upon the open book on the table and she read, "Inasmuch as ye did it unto one of these my brethren, even these least, ye did it unto me." In an instant her mistake of the previous day was made clear to her. She had been so busy getting ready for the Master that when he had knocked at her door she had failed to recognize him.

Picking up the book, she read the words which were so familiar to her, but which this time carried a richer meaning than ever before. "Then shall the King say unto them on his right hand, Come, ye blessed of my Father, inherit the kingdom prepared for you from the foundation of the world; for I was hungry, and ye gave me to eat; I was thirsty, and ye gave me drink; I was a stranger, and ye took me in; naked, and ye clothed me; I was sick, and ye visited me; I was in prison, and ye came unto me. . . . Inasmuch as ye did it unto one of these my brethren, ye did it unto me."

VII HYMN: "O Master, Let Me Walk with Thee."
VIII PRAYER: *(by leader)*
 IX RESPONSE: "Dear Lord and Father of Mankind."

## *May: Second Sunday*

SUGGESTED HYMN: "There's a Wideness in God's Mercy."
STORY:

### OUR MOTHERS

We observe Mothers' Day not that we may forget all about our mothers on the other three hundred and sixty-four days of the year, but, rather, that we may pause to say some of the things which are in our hearts every day but which do not often find opportunity for expression.

Some one has said, "God could not be everywhere and so he made mothers." Whether this is true or not, it is an attempt to say something which is true—namely, that a mother's love makes it easy for us to believe in a God of love. We know that God must be a loving God because he gave us our mothers. A Christian home presided over by a Christian mother is perhaps the greatest single blessing which can come into an individual's life.

Any one who has read the writings of Henry W. Grady, the famous Southern orator and journalist, has been struck with his sincere regard for the family relationships. He could hardly find words adequate to express his appreciation of the blessings of a Christian home. In attempting to make his viewpoint clear he relates how on one occasion he visited Washington, the capital of our country. As he gazed upon the magnificent buildings and as he saw the machinery of government in operation he said, "Here, indeed, lies the strength and greatness of our remarkable country."

Not long after this incident Grady was entertained in a humble country home in the South. There was an air of contentment about the place. Each member of the family had his allotted task during the day, and when evening came the father and mother and children gathered about the hearth, where they read a chapter from the Bible and then asked God's blessing upon the home before they retired. As Grady witnessed this scene he said: "I was mistaken the other day when I was in Washington. The strength of our great country lies not in piles of granite or in machinery of government, but rather in homes like this, presided over by loving, God-fearing parents."

Some may not have understood why Grady never tired of praising the humble Christian home, but the reason was not far to seek. Grady himself was raised in just such a home by a mother who loved her children and her God. He tells us that at one time, after he was a grown man and bearing heavy burdens in the world, he became very much depressed; the burdens of life seemed too heavy, the perplexities too great; his faith in men seemed to be failing.

In such circumstances Grady slipped away from his task and from the great city of Atlanta. He went up to the modest country home where he had been born and where he had lived through his boyhood years. His gray-haired mother was still there to greet him. He sat by her side, and she told him the stories which he had heard so many times before. She prepared for him the same kind of food which he had enjoyed as a boy. At night she took him to his old room, and he said his evening prayer at her knee. After a few days of this life Grady went back to the great city. Again he felt brave, and his faith in God and in men was clear and strong because he had once more gotten into his life something of the spirit of his mother.

Such mothers are worthy of all the honor and consideration which we can give them this Mothers' Day and on every day.

## May: Third Sunday

SUGGESTED HYMN: "Take My Life and Let It Be."
STORY:

## A SOUTH SEA HERO

To live freely and gladly a life of service for others, until it becomes one's chief joy, is the privilege of the Christian. It is not always easy to give oneself in unselfish, sacrificial service to others, especially when that service does not seem to be appreciated. There are some, however, who, like their Master, are able to forget themselves in service even when opposition, rebuffs, and criticisms meet them at every turn. Such a man was James Chalmers, the missionary-hero of the South Sea Islands.

If there ever was a fun-loving, venturesome youth, it was Jim Chalmers. He was not the sort of a boy whom you would expect to become a foreign missionary, but when the serious question of deciding his lifework arose he gave himself to the foreign field.

He chose what was perhaps the most dangerous and difficult field in the world, the South Sea Islands. To the work there, among those barbarian peoples, Chalmers gave himself with zest. The climate was dangerous. The people were cannibals. Plots were laid; his life was threatened; he was attacked many times; he was shipwrecked several times and often in danger of drowning; he was stoned; and his drinking water was poisoned. His wife died, and he was left alone; yet when the London Missionary Society urged him to take a vacation from his work and come home, he wrote, "If I am to have a vacation I would prefer to spend it in opening up the interior of New Guinea."

No hardship was too great for Chalmers as he tried to help the ignorant and degraded savages among whom he worked to a better life. At last, however, after twenty-one years of work Chalmers was induced to return to London for a time. It was while he was there that, in a speech before the directors of the society for which he worked, Chalmers revealed something of the joy which comes into the life of one who has learned the meaning of service to others.

"Recall the twenty-one years," he said, "give me back all its experiences, give me its shipwrecks, give me its standings in the face of death, give it me surrounded with savages, with spears and clubs flying about me, with the club knocking me to the ground—give it me back, and I will still be your missionary."

Chalmers had learned that the joy of serving others is richer and deeper than any other satisfaction which the world can offer.

On Easter Sunday, April 7, 1901, Chalmers's vessel anchored in front of a small island just off the coast of New Guinea. The next morning, amid canoes crowded with natives bearing spears, clubs, and knives, Chalmers started for the shore. His small craft entered a little bay, and there Chalmers disappeared forever from the view of men. A native afterward described what happened to the missionary when he and his young colleague, Oliver Tomkins, landed on that wild shore. He was struck down with a stone club and stabbed, his head was cut off, and his body cut into pieces and given to the women to be cooked and eaten.

Surely this was a cruel and revolting tragedy, but it was more than that—it was a glorious end to a noble life. Even Chalmers himself would not have had it different, for his death did much to break up the cannibalism of New Guinea.

A short time before Chalmers's death he wrote: "I

should not like to become a shelved missionary. Far better to go home from the field, busy at work."

The words contained in an address after his death expressed the feeling of thousands: "Know ye not that there is a prince and a great man fallen this day in Israel?"

## May: Fourth Sunday

Suggested Hymn: "When I Survey the Wondrous Cross."

Story:

### SAINT FRANCIS

About the year 1182 there was born in Italy in the home of a wealthy merchant a boy named Francis Bernardone. He was raised and educated in luxury. At a very early age he became the leader of a group of dissolute young spendthrifts in the community. His escapades were the grief of his mother and the talk of all the neighbors, but they were condoned by his father because his son mingled with the wealthy and aristocratic young set.

From one thing to another the young man went seeking satisfaction but never finding it. He knew that he lacked something essential to his happiness. He sought it in many places and, as a last resort, turned to religion. Filled with disgust at his own actions, he would slip away to some cave or grotto and there pray for hours. It was while he was in prayer one day that Francis caught a clear vision of the sacrifice and sufferings of Jesus and he realized that Jesus wanted his labor, his life, and all his being. He was filled with an overwhelming desire to share the burden which Jesus bore and to give his life in service to the needy.

Now, it chanced that in northern Italy at that time there were many needy. Beggars swarmed the roadside and the market place, and lepers and other unfortunates abounded. Francis had been used to luxury, but in the face of his new experience and of so much suffering he determined to abandon it all. To test himself he borrowed the rags of a beggar and all day long stood in a public place fasting with outstretched hand.

He left his home of comfort, gave away the possessions which were his own, and devoted himself to preaching and ministering to others in poverty. Where he could not give material aid he lavished his sympathy, and this was as much appreciated as his money. One day, at a turn in the road, he came face to face with a leper. The disease had always filled him with disgust and now he involuntarily turned away. Ashamed of himself, he turned back, gave the leper all the money he had, and then kissed the hand which received the gift.

Determined to follow the Master at all costs, and, incidentally, to conquer himself, Francis went again and again to the leper settlements, doing the most menial services for the unfortunates. He washed the sores of the distressed and on one occasion ate from the same porringer with a poor unfortunate who grieved that he had been cut off from his fellow men because of his disease; and, curiously enough, this youth, who had tasted all the pleasures of the world, found here in the service of the neediest of his fellows the joy which he had sought elsewhere in vain.

There is not time to tell of the many years which Francis spent in poverty and service. The life of this man has been written many times, and some day you

will want to read it.   No longer is he known as Francis
Bernardone, but he is called Saint Francis because he
took his Christianity so seriously and gave his life in
unselfish service for others.

# CHAPTER XII

## MAKING LIFE COUNT

### *June: First Sunday*

June is a month of unusual significance to the young life in our Sunday schools. It is a time for reviewing the past months and for looking forward to the future. The spirit of commencement is in the air. Ideals are being crystallized. Whether the ideal is that of the selfish or the unselfish life will depend to some extent on the direction in which the thoughts of pupils are turned during the period of worship in the Sunday school.

ORDER OF SERVICE:

  I  MUSICAL PRELUDE

 II  OPENING SENTENCES: *(by leader)*
> It is a good thing to give thanks unto the Lord. Oh, that men would praise the Lord for his goodness, and for his wonderful works to the children of men!

III  HYMN: "My God, I Thank Thee" *(school t. stand and remain standing until after the next hymn)*

IV  THE ONE HUNDRED TWENTY-FIRST PSALM: *(repeated in unison)*

 V  HYMN: "We March, We March to Victory."

VI  STORY: *(The purpose of this story is to empha-*

*size in a concrete way the inadequacy of material possessions in the face of the great realities of life.)*

## "DOES A MAN NEED MUCH LAND?"

It is not an easy matter for young people to determine just what are the worth-while things in life. There is so much wealth in the world and sometimes we live under such abnormal conditions with so much luxury and convenience that we forget just what is and is not worth striving for.

Tolstoy, the Russian idealist, lived a very simple life and out of that life he produced some philosophy which is worth our consideration. Fortunately he has put much of it in story form. Under the heading "Does a Man Need Much Land?" or "How Much Land Does a Man Require?" he has given us a story which contains much food for the thought of young people.

A certain man was promised for his own all the land which he could walk around in one day. Delighted with the rich prospect before him, he arose before dawn and, taking his lunch in a pouch, started on his journey. Before the day had hardly begun he was well on his way. As the sun rose higher and higher it revealed fresh areas of beautiful land, and the man kept widening his circle, determined that nothing desirable should be omitted. Rapidly the hours slipped away, and faster and faster the man walked. At last the sun began to descend. It became necessary for the traveler to turn his steps toward the place of beginning. He was far from home, and every nerve must be strained if he would complete his circuit before nightfall. The race between the rapidly sinking sun and the tired but determined walker became fast and furious. It was a question which would win. By a burst of speed, however, the man completed his circle just as the sun was slipping behind the horizon. He had reached his goal, and the land he had coveted was his. As he finished the circle he paused, grew faint, then tumbled over, dead from exhaustion. He was buried in six feet of earth, and Tolstoy leaves us to consider the question, "Does a man need much land!"

The parable of the Russian idealist is, after all, a parable of life, and its message is one well worth thinking over.

VII  PRAYER
VIII  RESPONSE: (*first stanza of* "Dear Lord and Father of Mankind.")

## *June: Second Sunday*

SUGGESTED HYMN: "True-Hearted, Whole-Hearted."
STORY: (*This story is designed to reënforce the idea presented last Sunday.*)

### THE MAGIC SKIN

Young people are always desiring pleasure and are often keenly disappointed when it does not come to them in full measure. For all the pleasures we get out of life, however, a price is demanded. One of the important questions every young person should ask himself again and again is, "Is this satisfaction worth the price asked for it?" Many of the things we think we most desire can be purchased only at a price that makes them undesirable.

There is an ancient fable concerning a skin which one might put on and secure everything that was desired. The only embarrassing thing in connection with the process was the fact that every time one wished for a selfish thing the skin itself grew smaller, until at last, just as every selfish desire had been gratified, it choked out the life of the wisher.

There are few things in life which one may not have if he is willing to pay the price. In too many cases, however, the acquisition of material blessings, together with the opportunity for the unlimited gratification of the appetites, narrows the sympathies and dwarfs all that is finest and most godlike in us.

There is a firmly grounded idea in the minds of many young people that being a Christian eventually involves the sacrifice of some of the greatest pleasures in life. Although, as a matter of fact, this idea is built upon a false foundation, it is true that Christianity involves sacrifice. We should, however, consider in the same connection some related facts.

Christianity involves sacrifice, but so does business, art, politics, and the professions. There is nothing worth while to be attained in life which is not purchased at the cost of something else. A man who would succeed in business must be prepared to give up indolence, ease, and personal comfort and give himself unreservedly to the task in hand. Arduous labor and oftentimes extreme physical hardships are involved, but if the end sought is deemed worthy, the price of success is never considered too high.

Sacrifice, then, is not peculiar to Christianity; it is a law of life. One may not avoid the necessity for sacrifice by refusing to become a Christian. Instead Christianity is the one guarantee that sacrifice shall not be in vain.  Many a man has sacrificed the finest things in life for money or honor or position, only to find that he has made a poor bargain; that he has squandered gold for dross.  No sacrifice which Christianity involves is ever in vain, for Christianity includes all that is most deep and real of peace and joy and success.

We may feel that in choosing the Christian life we choose to give up many things, but no sooner is the choice made than we discover that we have instead chosen for ourselves all the joys and satisfactions which a loving Father God could devise for his children.

## June: Third Sunday

SUGGESTED HYMN:  "O Master, Let Me Walk with Thee."

STORY:  *(The purpose of this story is to inspire the pupils to seize every opportunity for serving their fellow men.)*

### THE HOUSE BY THE SIDE OF THE ROAD

A poet was walking one day from one town to another along a country road.  The day was hot, and the walker was tired.  As he passed under the shade of an overhanging tree, he noticed a wooden bench and, fastened to the bench, a rough sign, "Sit Down and Rest."

Accepting the silent invitation, the poet sat down.  Near by was a basket filled with beautiful early apples, and again he saw a small sign, "Have an Apple."  The traveler ate an apple and, as he looked about, he saw a card on a tree, "At the End of This Path Is a Cool Spring."  The poet was thirsty, and the mystery of it all attracted him. He followed the path, and there he found the promised spring and a cup. By this time the interest of the poet was keen. He saw not far away a small cottage and coming from it an old man with a very kindly face.

Pressed by the questions of the traveler, the old man explained half apologetically: "Well, you see, a good many people walk past this way, and often the days are hot. We weren't using the old bench very much and we thought it would give some who were tired a chance to rest in the shade. Then when the apples got ripe, we had more than we could use, so we have kept the basket filled by the roadway. Then it occurred to us that the spring was hidden by the bushes, and that some might not know just where to find it, so we put up the sign to call attention to the spring."

The poet thanked the old man, and then as, refreshed and inspired, he continued his journey, a poem formed itself in his mind. The following quotation from the poem gives us its message:

> "I would live in a house by the side of the road,
>     Where the race of men go by,
> The men who are good, the men who are bad,
>     As good and as bad as I.
> I would not sit in the scorner's seat,
>     Nor hurl the cynic's ban.
> I would live in a house by the side of the road,
>     And be a friend to man."

## June: Fourth Sunday

SUGGESTED HYMN: "Who Is on the Lord's Side?"
TALK

### THE MAN WHO COMES UP FROM THE CROWD

Young people sometimes get the idea that all the big tasks of the world were done in the past. All the great discoveries seem to have been made, all the great inventions completed, all the great fortunes amassed, all the great books written. All the Pauls and the Luthers and the Abraham Lincolns seem to have had their day. Now there would appear to be nothing for us to do but to accept the world as we find it and to follow along the paths laid out in the past. As a matter of fact, no conception could be further from the truth than the one just indicated.

Never were there so many big tasks to be done as now. There are scores of millions of boys and girls in China without schools of any sort who need to be taught. There are other millions in India waiting and begging to be told the facts about Jesus Christ and the message which he came to deliver. There are uncounted tribes in Africa who have never heard of Jesus Christ. There are multitudes in South America and Mexico who cannot read or write and who lack the purifying touch of true Christianity. There are twenty-seven million boys and girls and young people in the United States under twenty-five years of age who are not enrolled in any church school, Protestant, Catholic or Hebrew. There are newcomers to America who have never had a chance to know a Christian American and who are still waiting for the touch of a friendly hand in the land which they have chosen to make their home. There are social wrongs in abundance which must be righted before any young person can choose with a free conscience a life of selfish indolence or ease.

Yes, great deeds have been done in the past, but greater ones must be done in the future if the religion of Jesus Christ is to be advanced in the world. Noble, unselfish lives have been lived, but never were the demands for unselfish service louder than now. There are problems before the church to-day which are as great or greater than any which it has ever faced. Will these problems be solved? Will the unselfish lives be lived? Will the great deeds be done?

All of these questions will be answered "yes" or "no" by the pupils now in our Sunday schools. There is no one else to provide the answer. If the answer is "yes" it will be because there are some boys and girls who are willing to do the hard thing, the unusual thing, the thing that demands the great sacrifice, the thing that may seem to involve doing more than our fair share of the world's work.

In the days of the world war young men and young women unselfishly surrendered positions, opportunities, personal comforts and friends that they might serve to the uttermost. Now the war is over but the great cause to which these young people gave themselves is not won. It must be won by the same spirit which, during the war, led so many to step out from the ordinary walks of life to do the unusual and the hard thing.

"Men seem as alike as the leaves on the trees,
  As alike as the bees in a swarming of bees;
  And we look at the millions that make up the state,
  All equally little and equally great,
    And the pride of our courage is cowed.
Then Fate calls for a man who is larger than men.
There's a surge in the crowd—there's a movement—and then
There arises a man that is larger than men—
    And the man comes up from the crowd."

It makes us wonder how many there are in our own Sunday school of whom it will be said, "He was different from the common crowd, because in a time of very unusual opportunity he forgot himself and did the great unselfish deed which so much needed to be done."

# CHAPTER XIII

## THE WONDERS OF GOD'S WORLD

### *July: First Sunday*

The summer season has its peculiar religious message for pupils of the church school. The service of worship should be planned with this thought in mind. The purpose underlying the following programs is to make God more real to the pupils by opening their eyes to the wonders of the world about them.

ORDER OF SERVICE

 I  MUSICAL PRELUDE

 II  HYMN: " From All That Dwell Below the Skies."

 III  OPENING SENTENCES: "The earth is the Lord's, and the fullness thereof. My soul shall make her boast in the Lord; the humble shall hear thereof, and be glad. O magnify the Lord with me, and let us exalt his name together."

 IV  HYMN: "We Plow the Fields and Scatter."

 V  PSALMS: (*repeated in unison*) The One-Hundredth or the Twenty-Fourth.

 VI  STORY:

#### THE TREES

A long time ago the poet wrote:

> "To him who in the love of Nature holds
> Communion with her visible forms, she speaks
> A various language."

One of the perennial joys of the summer is the opportunity which it brings for communion with nature and with nature's God. The beauty of nature stirs us to thanksgiving; its vastness fills us with reverence and awe; its adaptations to our needs convince us anew of the loving care of a Father God. From the study of nature we learn parables which bring to us moral lessons and we discover ways by which we can coöperate with nature in carrying out the great purpose of God.

Among all the works of God in nature perhaps none is more wonderful than the trees. For centuries they have been the objects of admiration and of wonder. Poets and orators have found in them an inexhaustible storehouse of fact and suggestion of which the mind of man seems never to tire.

Down in southern Mexico there stands a giant cypress tree approximately one hundred and twenty feet in circumference. It is said by many to be the oldest living thing on the face of the earth, even outranking in age the famous General Sherman tree in California. This cypress tree was several thousand years old when Jesus was born. It is as old as Archbishop Usher believed the human race to be. In its body it bears the marks not only of centuries, but of all the centuries since the history of man began to be written. Its trunk is indented and gnarled, yet it has withstood the attacks of man and of the elements and to-day stands out vigorous and strong. Its branches are healthy, and there is no sign of disease or decay among its members.

This tree brings to us to-day out of the past a lesson in optimism and faith. Surely no one could have seen the wonderful possibilities for growth bound up in the little sapling which began its career so many thousand years ago. The tree has not grown to its present size or grandeur all in a minute, but steadily, year after year, it has added a little new wood and a few new branches until it has become the giant of the earth.

Thus it is that we attain to the worth-while in life, not because we see the end from the beginning and not by a single leap, but by steadily and patiently making use of the opportunity which lies just ahead. Then, too, the great tree makes it easier to believe in the eternity of God. Surely, if he can keep a tree through all the vicissitudes of six thousand years, he can care for us in spite of the great mystery of death.

VII HYMN: "My God, I Thank Thee."
VIII PRAYER
   IX RESPONSE: "Dear Lord and Father of Mankind."

## July: Second Sunday

SUGGESTED HYMN: "There's Not a Bird with Lonely Nest."

STORY:

### THE BIRDS

The interrelation of the various parts of nature furnishes a suggestive field for investigation. Last week we were thinking of the trees—their beauty, their service to man. Surely they are one of God's great blessings; yet even this blessing is dependent on still another. Those who have studied the matter most carefully tell us that without the birds we could not have the trees. The enemies of the trees are many. If these enemies were allowed to prosper unmolested, the trees would be doomed. The trees furnish the homes for the birds, and in return the birds rid the trees of their insect pests.

Possibly no bird does more for the trees than does the woodpecker. Freeing the trees of the pests which attack them internally is the particular task of the woodpecker. We may understand how important this work is when we pause to realize how numerous the enemies of the trees are. More than four hundred kinds of insects are known to prey upon the oak, and many of these multiply with great rapidity when left unmolested. A single insect borer may stunt or even kill a tree. One woodpecker may save hundreds of trees from damage or death in a single season. One bird has been known to inspect eight hundred trees in a single day. At other times a woodpecker has spent several days upon the trunk of one badly infested tree.

Our birds, however, do not confine themselves to fighting the enemies of trees. They help the farmer by eating each year millions of weed seeds and, when given a chance, they destroy the enemies of the farmer's crops. Cotton-growers are said to lose one hundred million dollars a year because of the wanton destruction by hunters of quail, prairie chickens, meadow larks, and other birds which feed upon the boll weevil.

These gifts of God are more than mere ornaments. They, too, have their part to play in making the world a fit place in which to live.

### July: Third Sunday

SUGGESTED HYMN: "All Things Bright and Beautiful."
STORY:

#### THE FLOWERS

"Flower in the crannied wall,
    I pluck you out of the crannies,

> I hold you here, root and all, in my hand,
> Little flower—but if I could understand
> What you are, root and all, and all in all,
> I should know what God and man is."

God sends his flowers in such profusion that to the thoughtless of his children they sometimes seem common. The miracle of even the commonest flower is, however, unfathomable, and it is only our blindness that keeps us from the proper appreciation of it. It often takes some unusual experience to open our eyes. Such an experience a certain Frenchman had many years ago.

This man had been unjustly imprisoned, and as he trod the dirt flood of his cell his heart was filled with bitter thoughts about God and man. On the walls of' his cell he wrote, "All things come by chance." Lonely, miserable and rebellious, the prisoner spent his days. He had nothing to care for and nothing to do but think. Nothing unusual had ever happened during his imprisonment. Each day the routine of the previous day was repeated, until one day an event occurred which was destined to alter the fate of the unfortunate victim. Close to the wall of the prison, where the dirt was not quite so hard as elsewhere, a tiny green shoot thrust its head above the ground. The man, who without a tremor, had looked upon thousands of acres of green, was tremendously stirred by the appearance of this single tiny shoot. Here was something alive and growing; here was companionship; here was something to love and tend.

Very gently did the man stir the ground around the young shoot and with jealous care he watched it develop day by day. Slowly it grew larger and larger. A bud appeared; and then, as if for the individual enjoyment of the prisoner, it burst into a wonderful pure white flower. Already the man had ceased to think of himself. His thoughts were ever of the flower and then of the God who had sent it. One day he read the words which he had written upon the wall of his prison and he felt ashamed. He rubbed them out and then he wrote in their place: "All things come from God."

Finally the story of the flower spread abroad and after a time came to the ears of the queen. The queen became interested and after some effort secured the release of the prisoner; "for," said she, "a man who can love a flower like that is surely not all bad."

## July: Fourth Sunday

SUGGESTED HYMN: "Summer Suns Are Glowing."
STORY:

### THE ANIMALS

We live in an age of cities and of machinery. The automobile is displacing the horse; mouse traps, with their increased efficiency, are eliminating cats; policemen have replaced watchdogs; the necessities of city sanitation have made pets undesirable; even the wild life is driven out by the very buildings of the city itself. Gradually the American family is finding itself independent of the animal creation and is dispensing with it, or, at least, rendering contacts with it more and more indirect. In all this change there lurks a very real danger—the danger that the present generation of boys and girls will fail to learn the lessons which, for untold generations of God, has been teaching through the animals.

The wonderful ways which nature devises for meeting the needs of her creatures, the adaptation to environment, the compensation for handicaps, and the protection against enemies, are most suggestive of the ever watchful care of the heavenly Father for his children. The thickening of the coat of the horse and the dog as winter approaches and the shedding of the same coat when it is no longer needed would fill us with amazement were we not so accustomed to it. The soft-padded foot of the cat, which enables her to walk so quietly, and the sharp claws, which appear when she wishes to grasp a victim for food or when she must climb a tree to escape some enemy, are all evidences of adaptation to the necessities of life. The deer has little ability to defend itself, but it is made fleet of foot, so that it can outdistance its enemies. As a still further protection it is colored like the foliage among which it lives. The horse must travel rapidly over hard and often very rough places. Its hard hoofs enable it to bear its heavy weight without injury. The camel lives on the desert and is given a pad to keep from sinking into the soft sand. The long legs of the giraffe made it difficult for him to reach the ground with his head, but he is assured an abundance of food by being given a neck so long that he is able to reach much higher than any other animal. To compensate the elephant for his short neck he is given a trunk which enables him to reach the ground with ease.

The foregoing are only suggestions of the way nature provides for the meeting of emergencies in the lives of animals and for every apparent deficiency in equipment furnishes an adequate compensation. Surely a loving God will not do less than this for his highest creation, man.

This is only one of many lessons which the animals will teach us this summer if our ears are alert to their message.

## July: Fifth Sunday

SUGGESTED HYMN: "The Summer Days."
STORY:

### THE INSECTS

There is one entire realm of God's creatures which we rarely consider unless we are forced to give attention to it. In spite of this fact, however, this realm, the insect world, comprises by far the largest group of living creatures of the world. The number of individuals is countless, while the number of species is estimated at more than five million.

Ordinarily we think of insects as a nuisance and we would not be seriously concerned if we heard that they were all to be exterminated. Often their annoying attacks upon us make them seem the one blot upon the summer. It adds further to our personal irritation when we are told by the United States Department of Agriculture that each year the insects destroy more property than was represented by the annual expenditure of the United States for the National Government, the pension roll, and the maintenance of the army and navy before the war. The Hessian fly ruins annually seventy-five million dollars' worth of grain. The chinch bug levies a tax of thirty million dollars on corn. Hay is reduced ten per cent by the army worm, while cotton, fruit, vegetables, timber, livestock, and even manufactured articles pay a toll to the army of insects, which is astounding.

Although injurious insects destroy much fruit and grain each year, yet without other insects we would have no fruit at all. Practically all our fruit and all our most beautiful flowers are dependent on insects for pollination.

Insects are responsible for the rapid disappearance of decaying vegetable and animal matter on the earth. Insects provide us with honey, silk, and other articles of commerce. Insects, too, are the only agents which will keep injurious insects in control. In fact, we are told by those who know most about insects that their service is so great that without them the earth would be uninhabitable in a very short time.

As we think of the insects whose depredations are so many and serious, and yet whose services are so great that man is dependent upon them for existence, does it not suggest that for all of the limitations and sorrows of life there may be compensations in terms of a deeper, richer life, which converts even our trials into blessings?

# CHAPTER XIV

## OUR GREAT HYMNS

### *August: First Sunday*

The fundamental purpose of the leader's talks for the month is to assist the pupil in worship by permanently enriching his knowledge of our great hymns. Incidentally certain other ends will be served as the work of the month progresses. (For further details of these and other hymns see *A Treasure of Hymns,* by Amos R. Wells.)

ORDER OF SERVICE

 I MUSICAL PRELUDE

 II OPENING SENTENCES:

> "Make a joyful noise unto Jehovah, all ye lands.
> Serve Jehovah with gladness:
> Come before his presence with singing.
> Sing unto him, sing praises unto him;
> Talk ye of all his marvelous works."

 III HYMN: "O Day of Rest and Gladness."

> *(School stands and remains standing for the Psalm and the following hymn.)*

 IV THE ONE-HUNDREDTH PSALM: *(Repeated in unison. The use of this Psalm, as of others, should be announced one or two weeks in advance, so that those who do not already know it may learn it.)*

V  HYMN: "We Come with Songs of Gladness."

VI  THE LORD'S PRAYER: *(Or other unison prayer. Seated with bowed heads.)*

VII  STORY:

### SARAH FLOWER ADAMS

Just as we know a child better when we know his parents, so we understand a poem or hymn clearly when we know its author. A single meeting with a great author has sometimes lifted a whole life to a new level of interest. We may not all have the privilege of meeting authors, but we may know the stories of their lives and work.

Sarah Flower Adams is not the best known of women hymn writers, but she is credited with writing the greatest hymn ever written by a woman. The romance of her story began even before she was born, for her father and mother first met while he was a prisoner in a London prison. His offense was the serious one at that time of holding liberal ideas in politics. It was here that Miss Eliza Gould, a sympathizer with his views, visited him, and upon his release they were married.

Sarah was born February 22, 1805. Her mother died when Sarah was five years of age, and she was left with one sister, Eliza. Sarah was a poet by nature, and Eliza was musical, so Eliza provided the music for the hymns which Sarah wrote.

In 1834 Sarah married a civil engineer. She was beautiful, of delightful manners and conversation, and of exalted character. Even after her marriage Sarah and her sister were much together. Both died young, and the hymns sung at both funerals were by Sarah with music by Eliza.

Sarah's greatest hymn, which we are to sing this morning, is "Nearer, my God, to Thee." It became popular in America about 1856. In 1872 it was sung at the Boston Peace Jubilee by nearly fifty thousand voices.

Numerous interesting incidents have been connected with the use of this hymn. During the Johnstown flood in 1889 a young lady on her way to the foreign-mission field was imprisoned in her car beyond hope of rescue, and as the waters rose about her those near by heard her voice as she sang "Nearer, My God, to Thee."

As President McKinley was dying those at his side heard him murmur, " 'Nearer, my God, to thee, e'en though it be a cross,' has been my constant prayer." On the day of his funeral, September 19, 1901, at half-past three o'clock, people all over the land paused and waited in silence. Cars were stopped; street traffic ceased; and men stood with bared heads. For five minutes there was silence throughout the land. At the close of this period bands in various squares in New York City played, "Nearer, My God, to Thee," and the same hymn was used in countless memorial services held in honor of our martyred president.

Such are some of the associations connected with the hymn which we are to sing at this time:

"Nearer, my God, to thee,
    Nearer to thee!
E'en though it be a cross
    That raiseth me;
Still all my song shall be,
Nearer, my God, to thee,
    Nearer to thee!"

VIII  HYMN:  "Nearer, My God, to Thee."
 IX  PRAYER:  *(by leader)*
  X  RESPONSE:  *(by school or choir*:  "Immortal
         Love," *first stanza only)*


### *August: Second Sunday*

SUGGESTED HYMN:  "Speed Away."
STORY:

#### FANNY CROSBY

Of all the writers of hymns perhaps the one best
known to Americans is Fanny Crosby, the greatly-loved,
blind hymn-writer who died only a few years ago.
Thousands of persons all over the United States had
the opportunity of shaking her hand and listening to
her kindly words of cheer and wisdom.

She was born in New York State in 1820, and her
life lacked only a few years of covering an entire century.  When only a few months of age she became blind,
so that she could never remember seeing the sunlight
or the beautiful world about her.  In spite of that fact
she was always contented, cheerful, and optimistic.
When only eight years of age she wrote:

> "Oh, what a happy soul I am!
>    Although I cannot see
> I am resolved that in this world
>    Contented I will be;
> How many blessings I enjoy
>    That other people don't!
> To weep and sigh because I'm blind
>    I cannot and I won't."

At a proper age Fanny Crosby was sent to a school
for the blind in New York.  Here she graduated and
afterward became a teacher.  While still a pupil she re-

cited a poem before the Senate and the House of Representatives in Washington as an illustration of what education might do for the blind.

Although she became a teacher and afterward was married, her real lifework was the writing of songs and hymns, of which she wrote more than three thousand. "There's Music in the Air" is one of her best known secular songs, while her sacred songs are almost numberless. "Jesus, Keep Me Near the Cross," " 'Tis the Blessed Hour of Prayer," "Rescue the Perishing," "Pass Me Not, O Gentle Saviour," "Safe in the Arms of Jesus," "Some Day the Silver Cord Will Break," "Blessed Assurance, Jesus is Mine," "Saviour, More Than Life to Me," and "All the Way My Saviour Leads Me" are samples of her work.

Fanny Crosby wrote rapidly. Some of her best hymns seemed to come as an inspiration, with little effort on her part. She had a remarkable memory, which was of great help to her. When she was a child she committed to memory the first four books of the Old Testament and the four Gospels.

Some one told Fanny Crosby one day that a man on a western prairie had been attracted by the words of one of her hymns to a meeting which was in progress in a very primitive building near by. He had entered the building and heard a message which transformed his life. When Miss Crosby heard the story, she said, "If that is true, it pays me for a whole life of effort, just to know that I have had a little part in the transformation of one person."

The hymn that she wrote which we are to sing to-day has done much for the foreign-mission cause. It has become the farewell hymn for departing missionaries and is regularly used as they set out for their fields of labor:

> "Speed away! speed away! on your mission of light
> To the lands that are lying in darkness and night;
> 'Tis the Master's command; go ye forth in his name,
> The wonderful gospel of Jesus proclaim;
> Take your lives in your hand, to the work while 'tis day,
> Speed away! speed away! speed away!"

## *August: Third Sunday*

SUGGESTED HYMN: "My Faith Looks Up to Thee."
STORY:

### "MY FAITH LOOKS UP TO THEE"

Two weeks ago we spoke about and sang the hymn which is said by some to be the greatest hymn ever written by a woman. To-day we are to consider a hymn which is perhaps the greatest one ever written by an American. Its author, Ray Palmer, was born in Rhode Island in the year 1808. He became a clerk in a Boston dry goods store and later a student at Yale. He taught school in New York and New Haven, entered the ministry and held several important pastorates and one secretarial position. He lived to be nearly eighty years old, and his life was filled with worth-while work. He is best remembered, however, as a writer of hymns, and his most famous hymn, "My Faith Looks Up to Thee," was written when he was only twenty-two years of age.

At the time the hymn was written Mr. Palmer, afterward Dr. Palmer, was teaching school in New York City. The verses represented the spiritual experience of an earnest and devout soul. They were written in a small pocket notebook for the author's use in his hours of communion with God. Two years later Palmer was in Boston and by what seemed to be the merest chance met on the street Lowell Mason, the famous musician. Mason wanted a hymn for a publication which he was getting out at the time. The two men went into a store and there copied "My Faith Looks Up to Thee," which had been written two years before.

Mason took the hymn and wrote for it the tune "Olivet," to which it has always been sung. Shortly after Mason again met Palmer. On this occasion Mason said, "You may live many years and do many good things, but I think you will be best known to posterity as the author of 'My Faith Looks Up to Thee.'" The words have proved true, for, while Palmer wrote many fine hymns, this, his first production, is the grandest of them all.

Palmer was a most admirable and lovable man and a man of deep feelings. He tells us that he was so affected by the writing of his own hymn that he burst into tears when it was completed. He says of it: "It was born of my soul." Surely a hymn of such beauty thus conceived will not soon die. It has been translated and used in thirty different languages, and it has thus become a great world hymn of the church.

> "My faith looks up to thee,
> Thou Lamb of Calvary,
>     Saviour divine!
> Now hear me while I pray,
> Take all my guilt away,
> Oh, let me from this day
>     Be wholly thine."

## August: Fourth Sunday

SUGGESTED HYMN: "How Firm a Foundation."
STORY:

### "HOW FIRM A FOUNDATION"

Occasionally a famous old hymn comes down to us without the name of the author. This is the case with "How Firm a Foundation!" It has been attributed to several different authors, but no one seems to know for sure just who wrote it. It is now supposed to have been written by a man named Robert Keene. It was first published about one hundred and thirty years ago, and it has been in constant use ever since.

Frances Willard related that it was used at family prayers in her mother's home and that it had been similarly used by her grandmother and her great-grandmother. Thus, in one family this fine hymn had served the religious needs of four generations.

The hymn was widely used by both armies during the Civil War. It was the favorite hymn of the famous general, Robert E. Lee, and was sung at the great commander's funeral. It was also sung by request for former President Andrew Jackson in his old age. He remembered it as the favorite hymn of his departed wife.

On Christmas Eve, 1898, the Seventh United States Army Corps was encamped on the hills above Havana, Cuba. At twelve o'clock a sentinel from the Forty-ninth Iowa Regiment began to sing "How Firm a Foundation!" Other voices joined until the whole regiment was singing. Then a Missouri regiment added its voices. The Fourth Virginia followed, and all the others until, as General Guild said, "On the long ridges above the city whence Spanish tyranny once went forth to enslave the New World, a whole American army corps, Protestant and Catholic, South and North, was singing:

"'Fear not; I am with thee; oh, be not dismayed;
For I am thy God, and will still give the aid;
I'll strengthen thee, help thee, and cause thee to stand
Upheld by my righteous omnipotent hand.'"

## *August: Fifth Sunday*

SUGGESTED HYMN: "My Country, 'Tis of Thee."
STORY:

### "MY COUNTRY, 'TIS OF THEE"

Every child knows "My Country, 'Tis of Thee," and that it breathes a fine religious sentiment. It is not so well known, however, that this hymn was written by a Christian minister. Possibly it would be more correct to say that it was written by a young man preparing for the ministry, for Samuel Francis Smith was still in school when he wrote this hymn.

He tells us that one dismal day in February, 1832, he was turning over the leaves of a music book when his eyes rested upon the tune to which "America" is now sung. He did not at that time know that it was the music of "God Save the King." The idea of writing a patriotic hymn to fit the music came to him, and he sat down and within about thirty minutes wrote the hymn just as it stands to-day. It was originally written on a scrap of waste paper five or six inches long and two and one-half inches wide.

Dr. Smith said of it later: "I never designed it for a national hymn and I never supposed that I was writing one."

The hymn was first sung at a children's celebration in Boston in 1832. It has never been adopted by our Government as a national anthem, but it has been adopted by the people. Through it for nearly a century the people of the United States have voiced their love for their country and their sense of dependence on and trust in God.

The fact that the music of "America" is that of "God Save the King" has given rise to many impressive scenes. At international religious gatherings one stanza of each hymn has sometimes been sung and this followed by "Blest Be the Tie That Binds."

Dr. Smith wrote many other hymns, among them the famous missionary hymn, "The Morning Light Is Breaking," but he will be best remembered for the hymn which, as a student, he wrote in a few minutes on a stormy day in February and which, without any intention on his part, has become one of our national hymns:

> "My country, 'tis of thee,
> Sweet land of liberty,
>     Of thee I sing:
> Land where my fathers died,
> Land of the pilgrim's pride,
> From every mountain side
>     Let freedom ring!"

# CHAPTER XV

## THE BIBLE MEETING THE WORLD'S NEEDS

### *September: First Sunday*

ORDER OF SERVICE:

   I   MUSICAL PRELUDE:

  II   HYMN: "Praise God from Whom All Blessings Flow." *(Sung by school choir or by the entire school without announcement.)*

 III  OPENING SENTENCE: "The earth is the Lord's, and the fullness thereof; the world, and they that dwell therein. Oh, that men would praise the Lord for His goodness, and for His wonderful works to the children of men!"

 IV  HYMN: "O Worship the King." *(School stands and remains standing for the Psalm and the following hymn.)*

  V  THE TWENTY-THIRD PSALM *(in unison.)*

 VI  HYMN: "O Word of God Incarnate."

VII  STORY:

### DISTRIBUTING THE BIBLE

A boy born into a home supplied with wholesome running water may grow into manhood without once experiencing extreme thirst or having any appreciable sense of gratitude for the blessing which is his even without the asking. A person who has been lost in such a desert as Death Valley in California knows more about thirst and the value of water than ten thousand boys raised in city homes. Thus it is with most of our blessings, including the Bible. We have been told many times that the Bible is the greatest book in the world and that we should be very grateful for it, but the fact that we have never been deprived of the Bible tends to make us take it as a matter of course.

A little more than one hundred years ago in Wales a certain minister asked a little girl if she could repeat the text of his sermon the previous Sunday. Instead of making reply, she remained silent for a moment and then began to weep, saying, "The weather has been so bad that I could not get to read the Bible during the past week." The little girl had been accustomed to travel seven miles over the mountains each week to a place where she could get access to a Bible.

This scarcity of Bibles so impressed the minister, Thomas Charles, that it resulted in the formation of the British and Foreign Bible Society. This society alone has printed and distributed up to date more than two hundred and forty-five million copies of the entire Bible or parts of it.

It is interesting to know that the first Bible printed in the United States was printed in the language of the American Indians from a translation made by the famous Indian missionary, John Eliot, in 1663. In 1734 a German Bible was printed in Germantown, Pennsylvania, and in 1782 the first English Bible in America was printed in Philadelphia. Bibles were so scarce during the Revolutionary War that Congress ordered twenty thousand copies of the English Bible imported at public expense.

Some years later the American Bible Society was organized. Since its organization it has distributed more than one hundred million copies of the Bible or parts of it. Four different times in its history it has undertaken to canvass the entire United States and to place a Bible in every home. To-day a Bible may be had by any one for the cost of printing, and if this price is prohibitive, the Book will be given without charge.

All of this effort to place the Bible in the hands of every one has cost years of labor and much sacrifice on the part of many. Surely this thought alone ought to make us appreciate more than ever the lessons which we study from week to week in our church school.

VIII  HYMN: "Father, Again to Thy Dear Name We Raise."

  IX  PRAYERS  *(in unison.)*

   X  RESPONSE:  *(by school choir or by the entire school)* "Dear Lord and Father of Mankind."

### September: Second Sunday

SUGGESTED HYMN: "Faith of Our Fathers."
STORY:

#### READING THE BIBLE UNDER DIFFICULTIES

It is relatively easy to picture in our imagination a time when few people had Bibles, but it is not so easy to understand that at certain times it has been a criminal offense to own a Bible.

If the early Christians had used moving-picture machines, we might have had a film showing a Christian family rising early in the morning before the neighbors were awake and making their way stealthily by devious quiet ways and hidden paths to a cave, a cellar, a secret chamber, or even an underground burying place for the dead. Here we might have watched them as they sat quietly with a few others while some one took from a hidden chest one of the sacred rolls and read to the assembled group. After reading, a few words of conference, a prayer, and possibly a hymn sung softly, these early Christians would slip back to their places in the world of activities from which they had for a few moments withdrawn themselves.

It was dangerous to read the Bible in those early days. The Roman emperors not only destroyed thousands of the valuable hand-made manuscripts of the Bible which had been produced with so much labor, but they hunted down, persecuted and even killed those who were found with any part of the Bible in their possession or who shared in the group meetings of the Christians for Bible reading. It was an exciting experience to be a Christian in those days. One thing this persecution accomplished, however. It eliminated from the Christian group all those who were not desperately in earnest about their religion.

At the time of one of these persecutions, under the Emperor Diocletian, a young Christian named Marinus was serving as an officer in the Roman army in Palestine. He had done his duty faithfully and was about to be promoted to the rank of captain. Through jealousy he was denounced by one of his fellow officers as a Christian. Marinus was at once summoned before his superior officer and questioned. "Is it true that you are a Christian?" "Yes," replied Marinus. "Then," said the officer, "I will give you three hours to renounce your Christianity." Marinus at once went to the small Christian church at Cæsarea and told his story to the aged bishop. The bishop listened and then, taking a sword in one hand and a Bible in the other, he held them up before Marinus. "This is your choice," said he. Without hesitation Marinus grasped the Bible. He returned to his post, declared himself a Christian and, instead of promotion, received the sentence of death.

Marinus, like many another early Christian, learned that the things which are worth while always cost some one a large price.

### September: Third Sunday

SUGGESTED HYMN: "A Glory Gilds the Sacred Page."
STORY:

#### PRINTING THE BIBLE

Few events have been of more significance in the history of the race than the invention of the art of printing. For fourteen hundred years the Christian church had written by hand every copy of the Scriptures it possessed. If you will sit down this afternoon and copy one page of your Bible and then multiply the time consumed in the process by the number of pages, you will get some idea of the labor involved in making even one copy of the Bible. It is not surprising that Bibles were scarce and too expensive to be in the possession of the ordinary Christian.

It was a great day for the Bible when the first printing press was set up by Gutenberg about the year 1450. The first book to be printed on this first printing press of the world was the Bible. Since the appearance of that first printed Bible the printing presses have never ceased to turn out Bibles, and to-day, after more than four hundred years, the Bible is the best selling book in the world, and the printing presses can hardly keep pace with the demand.

In connection with the first printed English Bible the name of William Tyndale, known as "the father of the English Bible," should be cherished. While a young man in college Tyndale got hold of a Greek New Testament. As he read this book of which he knew so little, he was impressed with the feeling that the church had drifted far from the religion taught by Jesus. He was also seized with the desire to place a Bible in every cottage and palace in England. In a dispute with a so-called "learned man" about this time over the authority of the Pope, Tyndale said: "If God spare my life, ere many years I will cause a boy that driveth the plow to know more of the Scripture than thou dost."

Before Tyndale could carry out his project it was necessary that the Bible be translated into English, and to this task he applied himself. In spite of difficulties, opposition and persecution, the first copies of Tyndale's New Testament appeared in 1525. By this time both the king and the church were arrayed against Tyndale. Sermons were preached against him and his work, copies of the book were publicly burned.

Tyndale had been obliged to do his printing on the continent of Europe. The books were sent to England wrapped in bales of cloth and otherwise disguised. Tyndale himself was driven from one hiding place to another. To use his own words, he suffered "poverty, exile, bitter absence from friends, hunger and thirst and cold, great dangers and other hard and sharp fightings." At last he was betrayed by one whom he had trusted and was thrown into jail. Even here he continued his work of translation until October, 1536, when he was put to death by strangling after being condemned as a heretic. His last words were, "Lord, open the king of England's eyes!"

Surely this man deserves the title which has been given him—"The father of the English Bible." He, like Marinus, learned that the best things in life always cost some one a very large price.

## September: Fourth Sunday

Suggested Hymn: "We've a Story to Tell to the Nations."

Story:

### A LONG WALK FOR THE BOOK

If you had been in the frontier trading post known as Saint Louis some eighty-five years ago, you might have been startled one morning to see five strange, swarthy figures approaching from the west. If you had followed them to General Clark's headquarters in the Barracks and listened while they made known their identity and the purpose of their visit, you would have learned that they were Nez Perce Indians and that they had walked from the far Northwest, two thousand miles away, to secure "the white man's Book of Heaven." It was thus that they designated the Bible, of which they had heard from the traders and for which they had waited many years in their far Western home. They had been assured that missionaries would come to them with the Book but year after year passed, the old men were dying, and still the missionaries did not come. It was then that a council of the tribes was called, and four warriors chosen to take the long journey and bring back the much-coveted Book.

General Clark received these dignified messengers kindly, and for several months they were accorded the finest hospitality which a frontier town afforded, but the Book was not to be secured. The long journey, unaccustomed luxuries, and the tragedy of disappointment, each played its part, and two of the Indians died. At last the other two resolved to undertake the long return journey. Before they started, one of the Indians made a speech which brought tears to the eyes of many. He said:

"I came to you over a trail of many moons from the setting sun. You were the friends of my fathers, who have all gone the long way. I came with one eye partly open. I go back with both eyes closed. How can I go back blind to my blind people? I made my way to you with strong arms through many enemies and strange lands that I might carry back much to them. I go back with both arms broken and empty. Two fathers came with us. They were braves of many snows and wars. We leave them asleep here by your great water and te-pees. They were tired in many moons, and their moccasins wore out. My people sent me to get the white man's Book of Heaven. You took me to where you allow your women to dance as we do not ours, and the Book was not there. You took me to where they worship the Great Spirit with candles, and the Book was not there. I am going back the long trail to my people in the dark land. You make my feet heavy with gifts, and my moccasins will wear out in carrying them, yet the Book is not among them. When I tell my poor blind people, after one more snow, in the big council, that I did not bring the Book, no word will be spoken by our old men or by our young braves. One by one they will rise up and go out in silence. My people will die in darkness and they will go on a long path to other hunting grounds. No white man will go with them, and no white man's Book to show them the way. I have no more words."

This speech made such an impression that it resulted in the going of Marcus Whitman and Jason Lee as missionaries to the great Northwest. To-day the Nez Perce Indians are Christians and they are sending of their own men and money to help carry to others the "white man's Book of Heaven" for which they waited so long.

## September: Fifth Sunday

SUGGESTED HYMN: "The Morning Light Is Breaking."
STORY:

### TRANSLATING THE BIBLE

The Bible was written originally in Hebrew and Greek. To-day the entire Bible, or parts of it, are printed in more than five hundred different languages. The amount of patient labor and self-sacrifice which have been put into these many Bible translations is past calculating. Frequently from twenty to forty years have been involved in the making of a single translation, and the coöperation of many people has been required. One man worked fifteen years on a translation, only to have all his labors swallowed up by the sinking of a boat.

The mere search for words to express the ideas of

Christianity is enough to test the heroic qualities of the translators. James D. Taylor tells us that while the Zulu translation was being made, an entire week was spent upon the one word, "Glory." Oftentimes no words could be found for "sin," "love," "conscience," and other terms so familiar to the Christian. In the Chinese language no word could be found for "God." The nearest approach to it was the word "ghost." In Madagascar no word could be found for "purity," so the word "whiteness" was pressed into service. When the first missionaries went to work among the Nestorians of Persia, there were no words for "wife" or "home." In Tahiti no word could be found for "faith." At another time translators were perplexed because they could find no word for "hope."

The difficulties of Bible translation are not confined to those having to do with the expression of spiritual truths. How, for example, would you translate the names of the large number of animals mentioned in the Bible to the people of Micronesia, who never had seen a four-footed beast? How would you translate Isaiah 3: 18-23, with its references to anklets, crescents, pendants, bracelets, mufflers, headtires, ankle chains, sashes, perfume-boxes, amulets, festival robes, mantles, shawls, hand-mirrors, fine linen, turbans, and veils, to the Zulus, whose wardrobe consisted of a little bead work, a blanket, and a skin apron? How would you translate the many references to frost, snow, and ice to people on a tropical island, who never had experienced a temperature as low as freezing? The following is an actual translation in the Fiji Island of Isaiah 1:18b: "Though your sins be as scarlet, they shall be as white as rain." By mistake one translator made the people throw "thorn

bushes" instead of "palm branches" in the way at the
time of Jesus' entry into Jerusalem.

Surely the difficulties of Bible translation have been
great, but to-day we can rejoice in the fact that most of
the people of the world have at least a portion of the
Bible available in their own language.